Prais
The Art & Science of Loving Yourself First
'cause your business should complete you, not deplete you!

"What a wonderful—and timely topic! Only when we learn to take care of ourselves can we take care of our business, our families, and the world. This book is sure to give you some great ideas to love yourself . . . and your life."

-Nika Stewart, CEO GhostTweeting.com

"The book, *The Art & Science of Loving Yourself First,* is one that opens all your senses, allowing you to grow into the most beautiful, fragrant, blooming human being, to create your best life (both personally and professionally). All the authors do a spectacular job in giving you all the tools you need to be the best you were meant to be. Brilliant!"

-Margi Kyle, ASID, IDS, The Designing Doctor, DoctorMargi.com

"In a world that pulls at us in many directions and at a frenetic pace, we must take the time to feed our souls if we are going to survive its demands. This unique book, *The Art & Science of Loving Yourself First,* gives different authors' perspectives on the keys to their success, with practical advice and strategies that are sure to help each of us on our journey."

-Marj Henderson, Vice President, Cadence Bank, N.A., Starkville

"A refreshing and timely reminder that self-care is the greatest gift we can give the ones we love—including ourselves."

-Miki Strong, Lifestyle Business Strategist, Money Mentor, MikiStrong.com

"Loving Yourself First will take you on an empowering journey of self-discovery! This cohesive anthology, with actionable Self-Love Steps in each chapter, can easily fast-forward your business and life!"

-MaryAnn D'Ambrosio, MBA, PhD, Speaker, Founder, and Chief Inspiration Officer at LeapWithoutLimits.com

"In this fast-paced world, we have literally forgotten how to stop and smell the roses. Our fast-paced lives often feel meaningless. With technology, we have the world at our fingertips, yet in this 21st century we are feeling more and more unfulfilled in our lives. *The Art & Science of Loving Yourself First* gives you the tools and insights for turning your life into one of enjoyment, versus one filled with constant struggle and pain. We all have issues and things that happen in our lives. It's how you handle those times that makes a difference in your life. [These] tools are invaluable for helping you accomplish this. Well worth reading!"

-Lisa Copeland, The Dating Coach Who Makes Dating Fun and Easier After 50, FindAQualityMan.com

"I've been saying to clients for years—'Be the best you!' That all starts with being able to love yourself first. *The Art & Science of Loving Yourself First* is a wonderful resource to lead you into a way of thinking—and being—that allows for a love transformation to take place. You deserve to be loved by you, and this anthology is truly an amazing collection of authors, words, and great concepts. I can't wait to recommend this resource to my clients!"

-Kristi Fowler, Speaker, Life Coach, and Author, KristiFowler.com

"I love the way this book offers clear, simple steps to help us move into more simple living. What a powerful statement, 'What fire in your belly will get you springing out of bed in the morning with a huge smile on your face?' If we do not have that, we are likely complicating life too much! I feel inspired by these words, and I look forward to applying the tips offered as I move through each day. Thank you for a wonderful read!"

-Dr. Crystal D. Gifford, CFP(R), EmpoweredWealthyWoman.com

"As a Spiritual Entrepreneur, I am always seeking useful tools to grow my ministry/business to the next level. I found quite a bit in *The Art & Science of Loving Yourself First: 'cause your business should complete you, not deplete you!* The experienced business owners/authors of this wonderful anthology have left no stone unturned as they provided sharp insights as well as thoughtful exercises for the reader to complete, balancing practical wisdom and soulful advice. I was immediately motivated to make some shifts."

-Tonya Parker, Chief Visionary Officer,
MindBodyandSpiritWorks.com

"It's not often you find a book that touches on the importance of nurturing yourself while growing your business, and I've made the mistake in the past of not doing it—and believe me, you don't want to do the same. This book will ensure that you don't."

-Erin Giles, Business Philanthropy Consultant and Founder of
End Sex Trafficking Day, ErinGiles.com

"The important message for me in the reading of *The Art & Science of Loving Yourself First* is the re-realization that I am quick to put aside my desires, wants, agenda, etc. to care and do for others. In doing that, I don't take care of myself. I loved the sentence, 'And so it began, my quest for living my life on my own terms.' I decided while reading about simplifying my life, that I would again begin my quest, my journey, for living my life—fully. My life needs to be lived fully in order to fulfill my purpose. Living my life by doing for others, at the expense of not living mine fully, must stop. A tough-love message that I am grateful to hear once again."

-Lorraine Lane, Lane Business Consulting,
LaneBusinessConsulting.com

"At times as a business owner, you pour so much of yourself in your business you forget *you* as an individual. I enjoyed the simple but powerful reminders of the 'Loving Yourself First Notes' in each chapter. Each author gives you solid tools to help you get back to putting yourself first."

-Michelle Gill Newton, Author, Speaker, Direct Sales Coach,
MichelleGillNewton.com

"I'm convinced *The Art & Science of Loving Yourself First* to be an impressive blueprint for the architecture of life, in which we can choose to take active steps towards the release of our God-given gifts for the betterment of ourselves and others."

-Dan-ette Creveling Mitchell, Fitness Training and Studio Owner

"*The Art & Science of Loving Yourself First* is a must read. I don't know anyone who is not dealing with overwhelm in their life. This book takes you gently by the hand and shows you exactly how you can find simplicity and clarity in your life. Listen to [the] words of wisdom and start living the life you deserve today!"

-Sue Rice, SueRiceInc.com and Publisher of the Midway Café

♥

The Art & Science of Loving Yourself First
'cause your business should complete you, not deplete you!

Also by Splendor Publishing

Discover Your Brilliance

The Reframing Book

Out-of-the-Box Marketing & Promotion

Mastermind Brilliance

The Faith Walk of the Entrepreneur

Accessorizing for Design Professionals

Color for Design Professionals

Moneytudes

♥

The Art & Science of Loving Yourself First
'cause your business should complete you, not deplete you!

Co-authored by

Sherry Burton Ways, Sandy Conway, Rick Cooper,
Margo DeGange, Laura DeTomaso Smith, Steve Gutzler,
Amanda Sue Howell, Marybeth Hrim, Blaze Lazarony,
Nancy Meadows, Kat Mikic, Danielle Mohr,
Jane North Lyon, Lisa Rehurek

Compiled by

Margo DeGange, M.Ed.

Splendor Publishing
College Station, TX

SPLENDOR PUBLISHING
Published by Splendor Publishing
College Station, TX.

First published printing, August 2013

Library of Congress Control Number: 2013913842
The Art & Science of Loving Yourself First:
'cause your business should complete you, not deplete you!
1. Business 2. Self-Help

ISBN-10:1940278007
ISBN-13:978-1-940278-00-1

Business/Self-Help

Printed in the United States of America.

Artwork: © Celianna | Dreamstime.com
Cover layout: JMH Creative Solutions

For more information, or to order bulk copies of this book for events, seminars, conferences, or training, please contact SplendorPublishing.com.

Dedication

This book is dedicated to all the committed and inspired men and women entrepreneurs, with important and meaningful life-work, who don't always put their needs first, and who may have unintentionally depleted themselves or even pulverized themselves to powder in the name of success. This is our way of reaching out to you to say that we understand, we care, and we are here to help you do something about it!

♥

Contents

♥
Introduction

Many heartfelt entrepreneurs, leaders, and ministers—who are wildly passionate about their life-work—struggle to consistently make a living, make a profit, and make a difference, without pulverizing themselves to powder in the process! Once reduced to powder, we can easily be blown far away from our calling, purpose, and path!

So often, we make business (or ministry) harder than it has to be, leaving ourselves feeling burdened and depleted. Intellectually, we know that if we don't take care of the "CEO," the "company" will shut down. When we are worn out and totally spent, no one benefits!

To offer authentic and effective solutions for better lives to our clients and to those we lead, we first have to live it! We cannot ignore self and expect to be happy, productive, and influential.

Passionate people tend to keep going and going, and often fail to step back and take time for themselves. In their "full-speed-ahead" mentality, they may also fail to set up systems, and establish habits and rituals to help them achieve big goals while staying focused and refreshed. This results in on-and-off bouts of weariness and discouragement. Such well-meaning people (you may be one of them) end up extending themselves far beyond their limits, and sometimes beyond the point of mental and physical exhaustion.

The very nature of service is to give, and we know that to a certain degree, we *will* be "poured out" in our service to others. That is to be expected. However, we have to recognize when it is time to rethink, reposition, and replenish. We must recover from self-sabotage, and lay the foundations that springboard us into abundance and success. This book, *The Art & Science of Loving Yourself First,* shows you how!

For this collaborative book, I called upon the wisdom of 14 inspiring and motivating mentors from a variety of industries, who each contributed one chapter. These are people I know, respect, and deeply admire, whose lives are beautifully and purposefully in perspective.

As you read the individual chapters, you will discover that each writer represents a very unique vantage point, reflecting an array of beliefs and life philosophies, but there is a common thread: all of these mentors have reached a desirable level of success without giving away more of themselves than is fitting or appropriate. They have learned what it takes to run a business or do important work, without sacrificing their own calling, essence, or well-being. They show up here to help you love and care for yourself, while you grow your entrepreneurial endeavors, and develop your career.

The Art & Science of Loving Yourself First is full of truths, tips, and action-steps, so you can design a life that is whole and on purpose. Whether it's through simple business systems, clever productivity strategies, empowering self-care habits, strategic planning and reflection, overcoming specific obstacles, or serving from the right vantage point and for the right reasons, these pages offer you practical yet inspirational guidance and tools to help you contribute to your world—and lead—from a rewarding and engaging position of love, self-worth, and strength.

It *is* possible to reach high levels of success in your career while feeling energized and in control. You *can* attract the resources, environments, people, clients, sales, and money you desire, but to do this, you have to go beyond basic self-help, the

Law of Attraction, magnetic marketing, and impractical "fluff" about work-life balance.

This book will trigger positive shifts in your thinking about when, where, how, and with whom you work. It will allow you to take a serious look at what you want in all aspects of your life. It's full of surprises, too. Have you considered branding your home and office interiors so they become spaces that support your mission, goals and lifestyle? Have you laid hold of a healthy self-leadership plan that's full of hope, easy to do, and still yields peak-performance? Did you know that you can cultivate solid connections and foster meaningful relationships online through social media simplicity? Find your brilliance, navigate change and transition, set important boundaries, gain visibility, create powerful systems, build a team, deal with setbacks, turn fear into victory, live your passions, and manifest your vision! It's all in the pages that follow!

Right now you have a tremendous opportunity that I hope you will embrace with vigor. You can make the leap from reaction, frustration, and confusion, and move on to reflection, restoration, and clarity. You can renounce an existence of overwhelming (or debilitating) stress and a lack of direction. That's why we wrote *The Art & Science of Loving Yourself First: 'cause your business should complete you, not deplete!*

Turn the page! Open yourself fully to the self-respect and self-care that fuels personal power. Do what it takes to catapult to an elevated playing field, where you experience increased joy and greater influence. Decide to love yourself first. Determine to value yourself, and in so doing, you'll significantly impact the lives of others.

Margo DeGange

♥
About "Loving Yourself First" Notes

Working on an anthology with a group of writers is exciting and rewarding. It gives me the opportunity to get to know my colleagues in a deeper way. It also gives the reader access to a variety of thinkers on a particular topic. Each writer has a different writing style and an important personal perspective to share. This makes an anthology interesting. The difference in the styles and vantage points of the chapters also leaves room for a fitting method of tying it all together and forming the book into a cohesive whole.

My tool for doing this is to include my own personal "Loving Yourself First" Notes before each new chapter begins. These notes are my way of sharing the importance of the topics as they relate to self-love. In these notes I speak from the heart to inspire you and motivate you to make your own self-love and self-care a priority. Only then can you serve those in your business, ministry, community, or family. Never neglect preparing your heart and strengthening your inner and outer self as you go out to meet the world.

I will let you know here that I wrote the "Loving Yourself First" Notes for each chapter before I read what each individual author wrote. This was intentional on my part. I wanted to share my thoughts on the chapter topics independently of the other writers, and in no way speak for them. I think you will find the result refreshing.

Each chapter of this book has five components:

1. An overall message from me, relating to the general topic of each chapter, which I call "Loving Yourself First" Notes

2. A few personal words I share about the author of the chapter

3. A lesson from the author of the chapter, who is a notable success expert, a business person, and a writer

4. One or more "Self-Love Steps," which are simple actions you can take to immediately empower yourself

5. The bio of that chapter's author, along with a URL where you can learn more about them

I know you will not only enjoy this anthology, but you will be wonderfully transformed and your life-work will take on a powerful new rhythm from the intentional and meaningful words that make up this book—our love letter to you.

Margo DeGange

♥

"Loving Yourself First" Note on Gratitude

"Cultivate the habit of being grateful for every good thing that comes to you, and to give thanks continuously. And because all things have contributed to your advancement, you should include all things in your gratitude."

-Ralph Waldo Emerson

Filling your heart with gratitude is a giant self-love step. Being grateful feels really good and it opens a wide pathway for physical health and mental well-being. Gratitude is readily available and easily accessible to anyone and everyone, at any time, in every moment, and in any situation or circumstance.

When it comes to living an amazing life abundant in gratitude, the playing field is equal for all and the prize is totally available to each of those who want it, without exception!

When you are thankful you are agreeing that the big picture holds more than just you in the frame. With thankfulness in your heart you are always ready to meet the world and contribute to it from a place of purpose, meaning, and value.

Being grateful keeps you from feeling depleted and stuck. It is a choice to make, and once you do, it immediately fills you up, energizes your mind, breaks the shackles of your limitations, releases your potential, and pours refreshment onto others.

Choosing gratitude is the absolute best action you can take to love yourself first, and it doesn't cost a dime. This free and amazing resource will make you feel richer than a room full of grouchy billionaires, and more alive than a party full of beautiful people who forgot how to say, "Thank you for including me."

Danielle Mohr, the Writer of Chapter 1

Danielle Mohr is a woman who lives gratitude daily. Through gratitude she has found the secret ingredient to a happy life. Her loved ones and colleagues know her for it. One of our mutual business acquaintances referred to Danielle this way: "I love her. She is the most positive person I have ever met!"

Wow! What a spectacular testimonial! Could it be that gratitude has the power to leave a lasting and moving impression on others, so much so that they want to tell people about it? Is it also possible that someone like Danielle Mohr can show up today just for you, to encourage and inspire you to live more vibrantly and more fully? I think so!

Danielle is well-equipped to write to you about gratitude. It is her way of life! Take her words to heart and let them work to uplift your heart and mind. They can be the ideal map and lantern for your self-love journey.

Margo DeGange

♥

Chapter 1
Gratitude Starts with You

By Danielle Mohr, Relationship Marketing Specialist,
MCD, CCC-SLP

How often have you stopped to look around and feel genuine gratitude for your business, your relationships and the blessings you have in life? I believe being grateful contributes to your well-being and your overall happiness. When you take time to express gratitude, it changes your attitude, increases your confidence, and has a direct effect on others in your personal and business relationships.

My personal "aha" gratitude moment came when I began keeping my own gratitude journal. This journal and my ritual five entries of what I am thankful for have become a daily event (and, of course, an endless list). I list obvious blessings like my health, my family, and my community, and then I look at the "little things" we enjoy and often take for granted. My journal has entries expressing gratitude for pajamas, coffee, carpool, seat warmers, and color copies!

Some people are afraid to express gratitude, or feel guilty for wanting more from their blessings. I am giving you permission to be thankful for your partner, your spouse, your children, and your family, and permission to be grateful for your business and wanting to pursue your entrepreneurial passions.

"I've learned that people will forget what you said, people will forget what you did, but people will never forget how you made them feel." -Maya Angelou

Once you have gratitude for yourself and the things around you, it is time to express your feelings to others. My successes in both my business and personal relationships are because I take action and show gratitude and appreciation, and because I celebrate others today . . . not some day. Mary Kay Ash, founder of *Mary Kay Cosmetics*, understood the importance of gratitude. She taught her sales reps how simple gratitude goes a long way. The late Ms. Ash has a billion-dollar company and legacy as proof of her winning philosophy.

Thoughts and Words

Change your thinking. When you take time to start your day with gratitude, how can you have a bad day? I have personally experienced the difference of my focus when I start my day thinking about the things for which I am grateful, as opposed to when I start my day with negative thoughts. Negativity is draining. Making yourself write in the journal forces you to focus on the positive.

"If you think you can do a thing or think you can't do a thing, you're right." -Henry Ford

Unfortunately, children start to hear the words "No" or "You can't do that" from an early age. By age four, a child may receive 16,000 negative responses and over 80,000 negative responses by age ten. When you are grateful, your language will become more positive and powerful. You will begin to see the *Law of Attraction* in action and observe that whether you believe it or not it, the *Law of Attraction* works.

You cannot get in a good mood when your thoughts and words are negative; however, when you start the day with gratitude, your day changes for the better. So now is the time to start thinking, acting, and speaking in a positive manner.

"The name on the front of the jersey is more important than the name on the back." -Jim Craig

Appreciation

Nowadays, you see turn-over within businesses as employees look for other options. Not always do employees leave for bigger and better things. Some employees leave because they do not feel appreciated. No matter your business, you as the owner, manager, or upline are similar to that of a coach. Your employees, sales reps, downlines, and others within your company are part of your team, and just like any team, the performance of each individual player affects the performance and image of the entire team. Without simple steps of gratitude and appreciation, you will find yourself in a cycle of training new employees and downlines after some leave, thus costing you time and money.

In your business, first impressions are everything. You're building relationships. Be the person others want to be around. Be genuine and show you care during your rapport building. Don't just collect business cards, go the extra mile and write those thank you cards.

Do you send them a thank-you card, and a gift to say, "Thanks, you did a great job"? Have you ever thought what a boost your note of gratitude would give the person who received it? We all have an innate desire to be appreciated. You give those feelings to another with something so simple as a couple of written words of gratitude.

Self-Love Steps

1. Begin a Gratitude Journal. Challenge yourself to list three to five things every day for which you are grateful for at that moment.

2. Send a thank-you card. Do not think it is too late. Late is better than never! Reflect who you need to thank for a sale, a referral, or something someone did for you and your business. Send them a card today!

Nurtured relationships are something we all want and something we all should have. You need to nurture those relationships by making it a daily habit. Taking care of yourself with your daily gratitude list is the beginning of it all. Gratitude starts with you and then spreads like wildfire when you take time to show gratitude and appreciation to others.

About Danielle Mohr

Danielle was born in Vinton, Iowa and currently lives in Frisco, Texas, with her husband and three sons. She studied Communications at Iowa State and LSU Medical Center. Mohr's life motto of *"living for the present and not for the someday"* has been the driving force for her success as well as an inspiration for many. She enjoys working with a variety of entrepreneurs and checking off bucket list items.

Find out more about Danielle Mohr on her website: CardsandMohr.com

♥

"Loving Yourself First" Note on Your Essence

"The energy of the mind is the essence of life."

-Aristotle

When I think about the essence of any particular person, what comes to mind is our uniqueness. Your essence is your uniqueness, that footprint or fingerprint that is truly your own and that sets you apart from every person who is alive today, every person who has ever lived in the past, and every person who will ever be alive in the future!

It makes me sad when I see someone trying desperately to be like someone else . . . to dress like them, talk like them, act like them, brand their business or ministry in a similar way, and mimic them. I don't criticize; I am just aware that such a person has not yet embraced their brilliance nor stepped boldly into their true and influential (and God-given) power!

Being your true self every day is celebrating your essence. Who you really are is a precious jewel, and no two are alike! Radiating as that one-of-a-kind jewel is how you best love yourself and how you shine a light for others, and how you bless those who are privileged to meet and know you.

Never shy away from the true you. Don't believe that you are not enough. You are well more than enough! The true you is the gift we all want to see. The true you fills the world around you (and your own soul and spirit) with greater love. From there you will easily help and serve the people in your sphere of influence.

Your life-work is a mirror reflection of you! Love yourself first by taking the pressure off to be someone you are not, and love yourself first by being excited about who you truly and genuinely are! Then reach outward! Radically change lives for the better as you boldly and confidently meet others with your authentic self and your inspired, effortless essence.

Blaze Lazarony, the Writer of Chapter 2

Blaze, aka Barbara Lazarony, is truly a gift. She has that rare combination of gentleness and power that causes others to perk up and pay attention. Her soft manner complements her wisdom and undeniable strength.

This is an amazing woman who always has an important and timely message for those in her arena of influence, and at this very moment, that includes you!

Blaze Lazarony is on fire with purpose, and she can help you blaze a trail of self-love that will forever ignite your spirit. I know her words will hit you with a crackle and a sparkle to warm your heart, but even more, she will help you melt away and totally evaporate your fear of being fully yourself!

Margo DeGange

♥

Chapter 2
Embracing Your Essence
Brings Fragrance to Others
By Blaze, Aka Barbara Lazarony, Chief Visionary Officer

Imagine your favorite scent right now.

What comes to mind?

Perhaps the sun-kissed aroma of clean sheets snapping in the breeze, or warm, crunchy gingerbread cookies fresh from the oven? Or the gentle whooshes of a lilac perfume and a musky after-shave lotion that bring to mind dear ones from your past?

Your vivid sense of smell can recreate mental pictures in your brain, pictures so real that you almost can't distinguish fact from fantasy. This is one of the exceptional powers of our senses as human beings.

Defining the Essence of Self-Love

"Make me a fragrance that smells like love."
-Christian Dior

Your favorite aromas are individual and layered; they're a delicate infusion of old memories, current-day experiences, and future expectations projected upon your powerful sense of smell.

If you attempted to separate a scent into all of its distinct pieces, it would cease to exist in its entirety. The same is true of your essence. The essence of who you are becomes the sum of the many parts of you—your spirit, your emotions, your mental musings, and your physical body.

It's a challenge to define your unique essence, just as it is to define your favorite perfume. In the scientific world of scents, chemists use "notes" to describe the essential oils that are added to base oils, alcohol, and water.

In the pragmatic world of essence, we use adjectives to describe the qualities of a person.

Simply stated, adjectives are words that describe nouns. Adjectives themselves are not a total description of one's human spirit, emotions, mentality, and physical body; they are simply a starting point.

Self-Love Steps

1. Find a pen and piece of paper, and begin compiling a list of adjectives that you believe best describe you. If you find yourself stumped, ask trusted friends or colleagues to share three to five adjectives with you that illustrate your most positive qualities.

    As your list grows, you'll begin to notice trends. For example, some words may appear multiple times. Most likely, these adjectives are how people "see" you. Also, notice words that are slight variations of each other. As this happens, select the word that resonates with you most.

2. In the end, compile a list that contains five to seven adjectives that you believe best describe your essence. If you find that words are missing, feel free to add them.

Ensure that every adjective in the listing describes you in your highest, most positive light.

3. Next, take some time to get still and quiet, and listen to your inner wisdom as you review your list. This summary expresses the essence of you. How does that feel? Many of my clients experience a deep sigh of relief as they read the list aloud. They report that their sensory organs (eyes, ears, nose, throat, and hands) are in a heightened state, and that it feels as if their hearts are opening.

They are letting the love in.

You, just like every human being, long to be seen, heard, and acknowledged for who you are at the soul level. Knowing who you are at the depth of your soul allows you to love yourself just a little bit more in every moment.

Questions to Ponder:

♥ In this minute, can you allow self-love in?

♥ What, if anything, needs to shift or change to allow just a bit more love to seep into every cell of your being?

Embrace Your Personal Truth

"A man who wears a fragrant flower on his collar spreads a perfume wherever he goes." -Prem Prakash

As you begin to love your essence, everything in your life becomes more fragrant. Love is the answer. Answer with abundant love.

As you begin to love yourself more—the silly and vulnerable parts, the sad and edgy parts, as well as the fearful and joyous parts—your life begins to feel richer and more fulfilling.

As a child, you were taught to follow your parents' rules. As you entered school, you were encouraged to embrace the traditional educational paradigm, which may have meant listening to lectures, facing forward, and generally keeping a low profile. The same scenario may have existed in your religious upbringing, or within organizations of which you were a member in the past. Any or all of these situations may have sent your essence into hiding as you tried to be accepted or to avoid judgment.

By the time you reached adulthood, you may have found yourself attempting to follow the proverbial Joneses because you thought you *were* the Joneses! Many of my clients look at me with tears in their eyes as they complete their essence list because their hearts and bodies remember and embrace the truth of who they are at the core level. It's as if they've come home to themselves.

I invite you to translate your list of essence adjectives into both mental and physical pictures. Browse the Internet or your favorite magazines, or even take out markers and create a collage that is full of images that embody each of your words. For example, if one of your words is compassion, find an image of two people holding hands or with open arms. Or if your word is wise, perhaps look for an image of an owl or reading glasses.

Give yourself the gift of creative time to explore images, colors, or shapes that speak to you. Invite your eyes to feast upon all of the rich and colorful images you choose, and allow your collage to be the next step of living into the sweet fragrance of self-love and your personal truth.

Questions to Ponder:

♥ Can you release yourself from old organizational, familial, and societal beliefs?

♥ What, if anything, needs to shift or change to empower yourself to stand in your personal truth?

Living Into Your Fragrant Essence

"The fragrance of flowers spreads only in the direction of the wind. But the goodness of a person spreads in all directions." -Chanakya

When you live your life from your essence, you become a living example of the butterfly effect. Here's what I mean: by embracing the essence of who you are, you create small changes in the world around you. You automatically set yourself up to share your intrinsic goodness with others.

Many of my clients share with me that they have stronger connections to others after they have embraced their essences. In fact, embodying their essence encourages them to live a more abundant and harmonious life that's in balance with the truth of who they are at every level.

The truth is, knowing your unique essence can also help heal you and enrich your life and the lives of everyone around you. By embracing your essence, you become both conscious and fully authentic. These qualities are strongly magnetic to others.

Imagine being surrounded by people who complement, appreciate, and support your inherent gifts of essence. Close your eyes for a moment and in your mind's eye see yourself working with your favorite clients, earning great money, and living a life that you've always wanted. All of this is entirely possible when you live into the intoxicating scent of your personal essence.

More Self-Love Steps:
An Invitation to Exercise Your Essence

1. Review your list of essence words and your collage, and identify the adjective or the image that resonates with you most. It may be the sound the word makes as it rolls off your tongue that delights you, or the sensibility evoked as you trace the image with your index finger. All emotions and sensations are valid. Simply choose one word for now to focus on. You can come back and repeat this exercise with other words at a later point.

2. Find a comfortable position and come into the present moment by inviting in profound healing through the breath. Deep breathing exercises are slow and rhythmic, and encourage you to breathe fully into your lower abdomen. This releases emotional tension, calms your body, and brings clarity to your mind. Breathing is also a way to awaken an energetic connection with your experience of God/Source/Spirit/One.

    a. Take a gentle inhale through your nose, expand your belly, and fill your chest as you silently count to five.

    b. Hold your breath to the count of three. (Please honor your body. If, at any time, this doesn't feel good or comfortable, simply stop, and return to your normal breathing pattern.)

c.   Then exhale for five counts through your slightly-parted mouth.

Practice this cycle of breathing a few times, and when you feel comfortable and confident add in the final element of this exercise.

3. In the last step of this exercise, repeat the following word pattern aloud five times as you practice your breathing in the same pace for five cycles:

"I am (insert your favorite essence word), like/as (insert a visual comparison using a simile)."

For example:

"I am cheerful, like a thousand smiley faces." Or, "I am creative, like Pablo Picasso with flowers in his hand." Or even the slight variation on a theme, "I am as curious as George himself!"

Have fun with this exercise, and be patient as you guide yourself into your own distinctive rhythm of breathing and sounds.

Questions to Ponder:

♥ Will you add breathing and speaking your essence into your daily routine?

♥   What, if anything, needs to shift or change to empower yourself to share your essence with others?

Creating Your Signature Fragrance

"I'm totally on a mission to find my signature scent."
-Lexa Doig

Knowing and living into your essence becomes your own magic elixir! It is one of the fastest and easiest ways to appreciate and acknowledge yourself and others, and the more you live into it, the easier it becomes.

Consider focusing on one of your essence words for an entire week, setting intentions, as well as following through on actions, to become a living embodiment of the word.

For example, ask yourself the following questions:

1.   How can I share more (insert an essence word) in the world today?

2.   In what way would my business be different if I offered (insert an essence word) to my clients?

3.   If (insert an essence word) were in infinite supply in my life, what would shift for *me*, for *others*, for *the world*?

Feel free to create and pose other questions to yourself that help and support you in both your life and business. As you feel comfortable, layer in multiple essence words, as if you're designing your own signature scent with different notes. Perhaps your fragrance includes the sensibility of a sea breeze as it rustles through your hair, or the adrenaline-pumping cadence of expressive dance movements in a full room, or the refreshing, fresh scent you smell as you bite into an orange.

It takes experimentation and an overarching commitment to excellence to create your perfect fragrance. When you find it, embrace the sweet smell of success, and wear it with pride because your essence is brilliant!

About Blaze Lazarony

Blaze, aka Barbara Lazarony, is the founder and Chief Visionary Officer at *Blaze A Brilliant Path*. She helps Fire-Starters, Visionaries, and Luminaries blaze their brilliant path and manifest their big visions in order to light up the world. Blaze holds certifications as an Advanced Transformational Life & Business Coach and Intuitive Hypnotherapist, and is a sought-after speaker, workshop leader, and author.

Ready to feel the heat?

Find out more about Blaze Lazarony on her website: BlazeLazarony.com

♥

"Loving Yourself First" Note on Leading Yourself

"The first and best victory is to conquer self."

-Plato

It's so easy to look at others and know exactly what they "could" or "should" do to make their lives easier, healthier, better, more joyful, more profitable, or more respectable. Of course the "could" and the "should" are often subjective, and usually represent not so much the truth, but our skewed opinion of another human being!

Giving advice, directives, and orders to those around us can be a useful technique to avoid dealing with what's even more important, how we are leading ourselves. Self-leadership requires a significant effort on our part. It means taking the focus off looking at others and refocusing on how we can strengthen, renew, and empower self. It takes honesty as well as reflection and awareness. It also warrants courage to take the necessary actions to become the best you that you can be.

Leading self is loving self. It means you believe that you deserve to live your best life. Leading self is also the first step to being an example, a mentor, and a leader for others who can actually make an impact, and influence needed change. If you really believe it, you will *live* it!

Steve Gutzler, the Writer of Chapter 3

Steve Gutzler is man who means business, in the most authentic, loving, empowering, invigorating kind of way. He is a man of high integrity who cares about others. He practices all that he teaches, and determines every day to live and work on purpose, and continually become a better version of himself. He is a true leader, inspiring others through a very practical yet spiritual kind of vision.

Steve seems to know intuitively that the most loving thing we can do in life is to take care of ourselves so that we are available wholly for others. Steve takes care of his body, his mind, his spirit, his family, his business, his community, his friends, and his colleagues. It's not that Steve is always so perfect; it's just that he understands balance and boundaries, and has figured out how to quickly adjust them when real life comes along and moves the markers. Without sweating it out or missing a beat, Steve leads!

If there is anyone who should write about self-leadership, it is by all means Steve Gutzler. I am very proud to know him and to be his friend and colleague. Through these pages, you will get to know him too, and you will be the better for it!

Margo DeGange

♥

Chapter 3
How to Lead Yourself
to Powerfully Lead Others
Six Ways to Stay Strong, Healthy, and Fulfilled
By Steve Gutzler, Author, Speaker, Leadership Consultant

A few months ago I was working from my home office when my iPhone caller ID showed one of my favorite leaders was calling. I smiled seeing his number, expecting to pick up the call and enjoy a fantastic stimulating conversation and friendship with this world-class CEO. Instead of the usual confident voice on the other side, however, I heard a faint voice say, "Steve, I could really use your help. I'm in the parking garage struggling. I think I'm having a meltdown."

This once-dynamic and confident leader was now emotionally hijacked and paralyzed with anxiety. He had recently faced a series of setbacks with high level clients and was now facing a strategy meeting with the board. I quickly switched from friend and coach to a negotiator. He was being held captive by his fear of failure. The bigger issue was he was on a physical and emotional tilt. His leadership batteries were empty, and the fog of battle had dulled his senses and smarts.

After several minutes of personal encouragement, I had propped him up enough for him to face his meeting. My final instruction to him was to promise to meet with me the following week to regain clarity, vision, and life balance.

When we met at a coffee shop a week later, we re-crafted his purpose and vision for the next several months.

We created his preferred schedule, including:

- ♥ Fifteen minutes of morning solitude
- ♥ Coffee and light stretching
- ♥ Blueprinting his day to coincide with his vital three accomplishments
- ♥ Scheduling in a physical training session for the week
- ♥ Purposeful outdoor walking
- ♥ Once a week golf outings—his new passion and recreation

When our meeting was completed, I sensed a new man with renewed energy and hope. He had filled several pages in his notebook with encouraging strategies for self-leadership, sustainability, and life balance.

Now, take a moment and consider how you are doing in regards to personal health, vitality, and overall satisfaction. Do you resemble the broken leader from the beginning of the story or the revitalized one from the end? I can tell you nearly all of my clients, including executives, leading entrepreneurs, and personal leaders, have struggled to maintain a more balanced and fulfilling life.

Through my time with these leaders, I have developed many important leadership strategies. One of these strategies is about how to lead self to powerfully lead others. You do not want to lead on an empty battery or while emotionally depleted.

Self-Love Steps

To maintain your powerful leadership, here are six ways to stay strong, healthy and fulfilled:

1. Take time to craft a compelling vision

Our natural tendency is to jump into daily agendas and objectives. When I met with my friend at the coffee shop, we talked about his vision for his preferred life and career. I asked him what he really wanted to accomplish and what type of person he wanted to be. We talked about what was missing or being pushed aside because of his daily demands. I urged and encouraged him on the benefits of having a healthy self for becoming a healthy leader. It is not selfish or shortsighted to recreate and play golf. You could see the light in his eyes as we crafted a compelling vision for the next stage of his life.

I encourage you to take time and record your preferred vision for your future. My vision is about four pages in a notebook and when the fog of battle sets in or I begin to run out of batteries, reviewing my vision renews my direction and hope.

2. Soulful self-care

I'll never forget speaking at a university to a number of business students. In the question-and-answer portion, one student asked me what my number one point of advice was for them as they begin their careers. To their surprise I stated, "Do not ignore your soul. Do not treat yourself like a machine. Respect your body, soul and spirit. Renew your soul daily through music, meditation, prayer, and moments of gratitude. Learn to feed your soul like you feed your body."

3. Physical training

I'm grateful to speak and train around personal leadership subjects at events, and many of my coaching clients have emerged from these opportunities. When I meet with clients, we work on self-audits where we discuss seven key areas including relationship, career, personal development, finances, health and fitness, spiritual peace, and the fun factor.

Health and fitness is so critical because it touches on all the other areas. I encourage my clients to remember that it is easier to maintain good health than to regain good health. I urge all of my clients to see a personal trainer and a nutrition specialist. It may sound like a luxury, but in reality, the rewards are astounding.

Your personal self-concept along with a soaring confidence will enhance your leadership. I have even had one client who weighed over 350 pounds when we first started together. My leadership coaching motivated him to turn the rest of this life into the best of his life. He is now a fit corporate athlete around 200 pounds and he feels better than ever about his leadership, and his wife and five children are thrilled and proud of his devotion and transformation.

4.   Re-creation-al

I recently went golfing with the CEO from the beginning of the chapter. He had just purchased a country club membership and we were able to spend an afternoon chasing a little white ball around. The conversation was rich and meaningful. He is healthy, alive, and happy. I know not everyone can afford country club memberships, but whatever recreation you do enjoy, whether it is gardening, nature walks, fishing, bike riding, tennis, or boating, re-creation-al activities refill the emotional batteries. This is vitally important as emotions drive so much of our behavior and performance. We have all felt or heard someone say, "I cannot take any time for recreation. I am too slammed with work," but I recommend everyone keep in mind you cannot afford to *not* take time for recreation. Your leadership depends on a healthy and happy you.

5. Create a sustainable life rhythm

I love my morning Starbucks coffee. I'll admit that a little caffeine assists me in waking up and greeting my world. I have to say, though, that when I see people pounding back coffees or sodas to get through the day, it saddens me. I encourage my clients to develop a healthy work rhythm by focusing on work for 60 to 90 minutes straight, then allowing themselves to take a break to recharge, even if it is just a short walk around the office or a power snack. I also prescribe, if it is possible, for them to take a couple of naps throughout the week.

Personally, I like to do concentrated work between 6:00 a.m. and 10:30 a.m. Then, I typically take a break to work out and leave the afternoons for appointments with clients. Find a working rhythm that is sustainable and enjoyable for you. Your leadership will be more effective and meaningful.

6. Enrich your family life

Even the best of families and marriages are messy at times. I know my leadership is most effective when I have taken care of the home front. My wife, Julie, has been a rock and I owe her a lot for loving me, believing in me, and trusting me enough to begin my dream of my leadership business to develop and inspire greatness in others. She, too, deserves to be proud of her accomplishments in overseeing our non-profit Compassion2One. For us, it is the little things that bring us joy, like the Saturday afternoon matinees once a month, walking our two dogs together, or enjoying a bite to eat around Seattle.

We have three grown children—a daughter in real estate, a son in law enforcement, and a second son in sales. Our greatest joy has been to see their confidence emerge and to watch them become leaders in their fields. We have always been full-time parents and we still love our position. We have always encouraged our children to never quit, to be leaders, and to love. Our family is what makes everything worth it for us.

I hope you lead yourself powerfully with these strategies and encouragements.

About Steve Gutzler

Steve Gutzler is one of the nation's premier thought leaders on leadership, emotional intelligence, and personal transformation. As President of *Leadership Quest,* a coaching services firm that helps organization grow leaders at every level, he's worked with many Fortune 500 firms including *Microsoft, Boeing,* and *Starbucks.* He also works individually with CEOs, business executives, and leading entrepreneurs. Steve has developed effective presentations on team-building, customer service, and emotional intelligence for today's leaders.

Find out more about Steve Gutzler on his website: SteveGutzler.com

♥

"Loving Yourself First" Note on Hope

"Hope is the thing with feathers that perches in the soul and sings the tunes without the words—and never stops at all."

-Emily Dickinson

You cannot love yourself without being a holder of hope! Hope is the energy that shows up to encourage and remind you that the dream, concept, or idea in your heart is worthy to be there and therefore worthy to be fulfilled. Hope is the catalyst that gives movement to your purpose and drive to your vision.

Hope is more than wishing. It is an inner knowing and true believing that your plans are meant to prosper and that you are destined to succeed at what you set your mind and hand to do.

Hope is expectation fueled by desire! It keeps you moving, and even in the midst of appearing silly, foolish, naive, or overly confident, hope keeps you from ever being ashamed.

Finally, in a very real sense, hope is trust! One Hebrew word for hope, "yachal," actually means *trust*. To hope is to acknowledge that a presence greater than yourself is right there for you, ready and well-able to work all things and all circumstances to your good!

Marybeth Hrim, the Writer of Chapter 4

Marybeth Hrim is a woman who embodies kindness wrapped up in power. She is warm from the moment you meet her. That is just her nature. She really cares about others, and makes it her business to offer encouragement and hope whenever and wherever she can.

I firmly believe a true leader inspires and shares a vision about which others can get excited. Marybeth does that, offering people a vision about their own lives they can personally get behind!

I asked a mutual friend and business associate what stands out to him about Marybeth. He did not hesitate to say that she has an amazing compassion for people that comes from almost 20 years as a social worker. He went on to say that Marybeth has seen and heard every problem under the sun, and that she always gives people a sense of hope. She has that amazing gift of helping others feel they are not alone, that the problems they face, others have also faced and overcome! This is one of the many skills Marybeth brings to her leadership coaching.

Margo DeGange

♥

Chapter 4
Leading Confidently through H.O.P.E.
By Marybeth Hrim, Leadership Consultant, LCSW, MBA

The world is a noisy place. Unfortunately, a magic wand isn't available to take away the confusion and clutter of modern life that can keep us from being and doing our best, but there is HOPE. If you focus on the following four building blocks I will share with you here, you can start confidently towards the ultimate goal of becoming a success.

Technology has made it easy to "reach out and touch someone" every second of the day. Business communities have many people who claim they can solve any issue that may be troubling you. This bottled and pre-fabricated success has become so popular it's in our business, relationships, and our personal happiness. The need to be liked and respected is a necessity in business. "Like my _____ on Facebook" is now standard copy on almost every communication.

It's a fact people do business with people they know, like, and trust. Unfortunately, our "always on," impersonal, and anonymous Internet culture has helped to mask who we really are and erode our true self-image. We compromise on core values and beliefs, allowing our avatar to represent us and assume a more comfortable pragmatic role. We also often engage too much and too often, at our own expense. When this happens, we lose ourselves. Confusion and fear sets in and our confidence in routine decisions is second-guessed.

Have you experienced any of these feelings? If you have, you are in luck. I will discuss four ways to keep your business and life simple. This strategy will keep you centered and focused and help you not only take care of yourself, but also make better decisions with confidence. Leadership is simply influence. We all have influence, but we need to learn how to utilize it effectively.

It begins with taking care of you. I have taken many trips on an airplane for business and pleasure. Before take-off, the flight attendants run through their pre-flight instructions. The announcer states, "In the event we lose cabin pressure, four oxygen masks will fall. Please put your oxygen mask on first before assisting others." When doing business, do you forget to put the oxygen mask on yourself first?

Lending a hand to customers is important, but taking care of you and your business is critical to your future. Ever say to yourself, "I hope today goes better than yesterday," or "I hope I don't have to deal with an angry customer today"? The word hope is used a lot in language. Hope is one of the keys to persuasion, and a very powerful emotional trigger. The good news is there is HOPE! Yes, hope.

The way to keep your business focused, and simplify your life, is through H.O.P.E.

There are four parts to it:

- ♥ **Harmony**
- ♥ **Original**
- ♥ **Purpose**
- ♥ **Empower**

The power of this four-part H.O.P.E. system will take you to a level of growth you have only dreamed about. It will help you tame the fear you have of yourself so you can begin to not only take care of you, but love you! There is a need to find the greatness inside you. Hope will help you connect to YOU with a greater passion for what you do and the talents you bring to the world. You were put here on this earth for a greater purpose, much grander than you can ever imagine. You know what is deep in your heart. Hope will help you to not only achieve it, but grow and maintain it.

We tend to get stuck in life and feel alone. The H.O.P.E. system will help you get unstuck and take care of yourself the way you need to, so you can take care of business! Let's begin the journey of HOPE.

Are you ready? Buckle your seatbelts. We are about to blast off for a ride of a lifetime!

Harmony

"Harmony makes small things grow; lack of it makes great things decay." –Sallust

Conditions and circumstances creep up and can make life uncomfortable. Some days feel out-of-sync, not in harmony with how you want to live. You feel disconnected from yourself and the world. Cultivating harmony in your business and life is important.

Self-Love Step

Firstly, you need to ask yourself some tough self-discovery questions, such as:

- ♥ What type of people do I attract?
- ♥ What do I enjoy doing?
- ♥ Where do I enjoy working (indoors/outdoors)?
- ♥ Would I say a glass is half empty or half full?

These are classic questions that you would find in a personality or skills assessment. They may seem simplistic and the answers obvious, but it is really important to know yourself!

"It is said that if you know your enemies and know yourself, you will not be imperiled in a hundred battles; if you do not know your enemies, but do know yourself, you will win one and lose one; if you do not know your enemies nor yourself, you will be imperiled in every single battle."
-Sun Tzu

It was true in ancient times and ever truer today. We must know what is going on inside to be effective in battle or in life.

When you listen to a piece of music, and all the sounds are in perfect alignment, and a beautiful arrangement is created, does it bring you joy? Do you feel joy when the strings bring a gentle sound to your ear, or when the brass section rivets a herald which makes your stomach do flip flops, or when you hear the thunder of the drums driving a powerful rhythm that keeps going on and on? All of these sounds connect to become a source of harmonious music. When played together, with each instrument appropriate to their purpose, they are in sync with each other. These sounds make wonderful music.

In our lives and businesses, we play beautiful music with our thoughts, opinions, beliefs, and values. You bring a harmonious connection to your life and to others. You matter!

As I look back on my life and the chaos I've experienced, I have become very aware of my circumstances. Many years ago, I married young and had children right away. They certainly were a precious gift given to me, but I knew I wanted to do and be more. My life seemed out-of-sync because I had no idea what was in store for me.

After my second child was born, I made the decision to pursue a degree in social work. Ever since I was young I knew helping people was the path in my life. As soon as I entered school I knew I was in the right place, and life was back in harmony. Achieving my degree was a huge milestone; I later went on and received my master's degree and eventually became licensed to practice as a therapist. This was a time of my life that was in harmony with everything I wanted to do. I was connected to who I was. Harmony does this. It connects you to yourself! Achieving those milestones produced a sense of peace and harmony inside me. It was the perfect music playing in my life and business.

Do you want inner peace, and harmony within yourself? I believe what we do in our business can create this harmony when it's what we were meant to do. However, there are days it doesn't seem very peaceful, and as a matter of fact, at times it's a struggle. Cultivating harmony is not an easy thing to do. You have to remember that every day is a gift and you can only do the best you can do. It's about growth and decision-making. I found out a long time ago, that the decisions I make in my business and in my life, create an abundance of either harmony or disharmony. One of my mentors told me that what I think about "shows up perfectly and abundantly." Wow! How true!

It's our thoughts that provide our state of mind. Our internal computer spits out new programming every day, which determines our actions and behavior. Harmony is nature's signal for growth. If you can become aware of your internal thinking, the external noises and struggles tend to dwindle down to nothing.

Self-Love Step

You can transform your life into a more peaceful harmony by listening to yourself and paying attention to the good thoughts you have about you. Start small and watch it grow and build into beautiful music. It's the little things that bring peace and harmony.

Original

> *"If you want to be original just try being yourself,*
> *because God has never made two people exactly alike."*
> -Bernard Meltzer

Ever wish you could be a great artist, musician, athlete, or leader? I think we all dream at times of being like someone else. You certainly are one of a kind. No one at all has the talents you have. You are an original piece of art. One of my personal mentors, John Maxwell, states, *"You always want to work in your gift zone."*

How do you utilize these gifts to your advantage? The most important relationship you will ever have is with yourself, and it is also one of the hardest! It's so easy getting to know another human being. You can see their behavior and feel their body language. This is why we want what others have, because we can see it. It's much more difficult to do that for yourself. You would literally have to carry a mirror with you 24/7! Who you are will reflect in your business and life.

Originality begins with a sense of peace about you. In my work as a social worker, I found that the number one issue for people was the relationship they had with themselves. You don't come with a handbook the day you are born, so through your life you need to explore the nature of you. In business, the failures come when you aren't concentrating on creating the best version of you. In his book, Good to Great, Jim Collins describes this process as the *"Hedgehog Principle."*

> *". . . the hedgehog remains safe because it knows that it is better than anyone else at one thing: curling up into a ball of spikes."*

Self-Love Step

You need to ask yourself, "What are my best talents?" It wouldn't make any sense for a gazelle to behave like a hedgehog; it doesn't have a spiny suit of armor for a coat. A gazelle would be a convenient cheetah snack if it attempted to curl into a ball instead of focusing on running faster and farther than its pursuer.

Applying the lesson from Harmony, we should have a good idea about the inner "me" and the gifts, abilities, dreams, and aspirations that we will use as our "Original" equipment, as we assemble the HOPE acronym. It is vital to focus your effort on your strengths. In business school the *Pareto Principle* is one of the essential conceptual frameworks that is often repeated, "20 percent are vital and 80 percent are trivial." This is an important concept that applies to many areas of life. It is essential that we identify the 20 percent of what we do best and dedicate at least 80 percent of our resources towards that strength. The clarity will come if you spend the time needed to identify these areas. There really is only one of you! You deserve the time and energy it takes to get to know the original you.

Purpose

"The purpose of life is to live it, to taste experience to the utmost, to reach out eagerly and without fear for newer and richer experience." -Eleanor Roosevelt

This quote from Eleanor Roosevelt is one on which to intentionally reflect. Have you ever been asked the question, "What is your purpose in life?" I have been asked this question many times. It's a question I ask myself quite often. What I have realized is that purpose is not external. It's not something I do or even have. It really has nothing to do with what I do well in business.

Purpose is an inside job! It comes from the heart. Once you understand it, it makes you whole. You must work from the inside out in order to reach your purpose. This requires you to dig deep. This, my friend, is a very difficult task.

When you ask yourself, "Why do I exist?" and really spend many months pondering this question and asking others for counsel, eventually the light bulb turns on. Most people just don't spend the quality time to do this. This question is an everyday question you should ask yourself. Why do I exist? Rick Warren's book, "The Purpose-Driven Life," takes a biblical perspective to both ask and answer the question. Spiritual belief is not essential for everybody, but a philosophy that conforms to your world view is necessary to approach closure on this question.

The "why" has become popular as an alternative to the lofty mission statements of 20 years ago. Simon Sinek has been speaking on "why" with great success. In his Golden Circle explanation of the "why" behind Apple Computer, he lays out a compelling use of the "why" when he said, "People don't buy what you do, they buy why you do it."

You see, hope and confidence is a choice. In order to begin to look inward you must first choose to do the heavy lifting. I have been a serious student of personal development for over 30 years. When I first began my journey into finding my true purpose, it was not easy. After 15 of those years searching for the answers, I realized the answer I was seeking was locked inside. My purpose of a full business and life did not come from others, it came from me.

Self-Love Step

You have the key to your purpose. It requires you to look inward daily and ask yourself the tough question, is this really who I am?   When we seek within ourselves, the answer appears. Then the "original you" arrives. Seek purpose daily and confidently.

Empowerment

"You are the master of your destiny. You can influence, direct, and control your own environment. You can make your life what you want it to be." -Napoleon Hill

Leading confidently through HOPE in a noisy world can be challenging. You have what it takes to navigate your business and life. The last of the HOPE system is Empowerment. Thus far the three ingredients of HOPE were all on finding yourself. It started with Harmony, then Originality, and then Purpose.

Empowerment is taking control of your business and life in order to achieve the first three essentials of HOPE. It's also the ability to recognize what is good in your business and life. Celebrate the small victories. There are times we are unable to see our small accomplishments in business and life, and this can hold us back from being joyful.

Empowering yourself is seeing the small feats in life and being grateful for them. Even in failures, celebrate with confidence and move forward. There was a time I felt all defeat in my business. I felt I was going backwards and nothing worked. I tried every avenue and turned every corner. I felt like giving up.

One day I sat and talked with a great mentor of mine. He stated, "Going backwards is a way to move forward." Ever watch the summer Olympics? The high jump has always fascinated me. The participants in the jump move backwards first. This gives them the ability to look forward and gives them a good running start. They never begin running forward, hit the jump ramp, and up and over they go. No, they move backwards to get a clear view. That's exactly how you empower yourself!

Self-Love Step

Just move backwards! Get a good view of what is in front, and then full steam ahead! There is always hope isn't there? We can lead ourselves confidently and joyfully through any process. You indeed are the captain of your ship.

Conclusion

Having Hope in our business and personal life is so important. It begins with a connection within you. Taking care of you can be challenging, but with the H.O.P.E system it's more than possible on a daily basis. You can learn to not only love yourself in a way that will help you be successful, but you can also learn to handle well the times that are most difficult. Hope is about growing the original you and creating beautiful music. This helps you ignite your passion in business and in life. Hope creates a peace when times are rough. Harmony, Original, Purpose, and Empower are the keys to hope. H.O.P.E guides you to lead confidently!

About Marybeth Hrim

Marybeth Hrim is a Certified Coach with *The John Maxwell Team*, an international organization committed to developing leaders. She's a teacher and speaker with over 18 years experience helping people achieve their maximum potential. She helps companies and individuals cultivate harmony. She believes creating harmony in life, family, and business leads to an abundance of peace. Marybeth holds a Master's Degree in both Social Work and Business Administration with a concentration in Leadership.

Find out more about Marybeth Hrim on her website: MBHrim.com

♥

"Loving Yourself First" Note on Your Passion

"There is no passion to be found playing small—in settling for a life that is less than the one you are capable of living."

-Nelson Mandela

I believe one of the greatest ways you can love yourself first is to invest time doing what you are most passionate about. When you create an avenue for the thing that makes you light up and really come alive, life and work have much greater meaning.

There seems to be a lot of talk on passion, and it makes sense because your passion has a way of connecting you to that innermost part of yourself that is true and sincere.

If you are to live abundantly and joyfully, you must invest time, energy, and resources in what you love to do. If you love to write, for example, you could create a sacred writing space and reserve time to be in that space each week, scheduling it in advance. If biking is your thing, you could reserve a portion of your weekends for a glorious ride. Don't ever let yourself become so busy with the "necessary things" and life routines that you neglect to fan the flames of your aliveness.

If at all possible, do for a living the thing you are most passionate about. Again, if you love to write, consider being a copy editor or an author. Or, if numbers are your thing, bookkeeping or business planning may be options for you. If you love to encourage and inspire, and you get uber excited about communicating important life or business principles, then perhaps public speaking, workshop leading, or coaching may be some ways you can serve others through your passion.

Sometimes, we are not very skilled at the thing we are most passionate about, so doing it for a living is not an option, at least not yet. What then? Let's say you absolutely love to sing, and dream of singing for a living but you really don't have much talent there. You have a few options:

1. You can get additional training until you are skilled enough to make it your occupation (your passion in this area will motivate you to grow, learn and become better at your craft).

2. You can find a career that relates strongly to your passion, but where high skills in your specific passion-area are not required. For example, someone passionate about singing, but not skilled at it, could become a manager for singers, or perhaps a writer of commercial jingles. Find an area related to your passion.

3. You can choose a business, niche, ministry, or career area that correlates to something in which you are both highly skilled and very interested (even though it may not be your highest passion) and leave the mega-passion area for your recreational time. The great thing about this option is that through your rich skills, you will be creating the funds to regularly invest in your passion.

For a successful career, you must be very skilled at what you do, not simply passionate about it, but you also should avoid a career that you are good at but hate doing. That is no way to live. It isn't motivating and it drains your energy sources.

If making a living doing what you are most passionate about is not an option because of low skills, look for that brilliant sweet-spot where your highest skills-set and your greatest natural abilities intersect with one of your great interest areas, and focus on this as a career field. If that intersection means your most intense passion is not what you make money doing right now, go with the next greatest passion that you are really good at doing. Once you grow in skill you can adjust your career focus, and in the meantime you can engage in your utmost passion on the side. The most important thing is to always make ample room in your daily life for your most intense passions on a regular basis.

Kat Mikic, the Writer of Chapter 5

Kat Mikic is a vibrant, positive, soul-filled woman who has made it her life's mission to help others grow and succeed. Kat has been faced with a number of giant obstacles that would have caused many to give up and go home, but not Kat! She is an abundance-manifester who just won't quit, and why should she? Her gift of brilliance is a beaming light that shines on others to help them out of the darkness!

Kat has a fun personality, and it comes through even online or in printed pages. You just have to love this gal! You cannot help but love her once you see her in action!

As if being an overcomer, a positive force, and loads of fun weren't enough, Kat is also very skilled and knowledgeable at her craft. She can help any business owner create an authentic presence online that appeals to just the right clients. I think this woman is a true gem. I know you will too!

Margo DeGange

♥

Chapter 5
The Art & Science of
Manifesting Your True Passion
By Kat Mikic, Online Marketing and Life Coach

It was supposed to be your ticket to freedom. You weren't unrealistic about it. You knew it would take time and a great deal of work, but you're feeling like you're trying to be the best of everything to everyone.

From a technological viewpoint things are changing so rapidly, you probably feel like you just master one thing when it all changes, and that there's still always so much more to learn and do. You have created your vision board and you know exactly what you want to accomplish, but to be honest, it's challenging, and you're more than likely feeling tired and worn down.

I know you, I feel you. I have been there and so has every single one of my clients. So how do you turn it all around so that your business not only supports you financially but also soulfully? How do you turn it around so that you are 100 percent aligned with your passion, working with your power and in flow?

I'm going to help you reconnect with your higher vision and purpose, because once we are back in check with who we are and what we really want, marketing our business, attracting clients, and manifesting our true vision and passion becomes easier, and the stress levels decrease. It's all about you, and putting your true self back into your business.

Today I will help you lay the foundation to a marketing launch plan and also give you some steps to execution so that you can truly create and manifest a passion business that ignites your soul and makes a difference in the world.

Purpose

Why is it that you do what you do? Why did you start it all in the first place? I have found that if we are not connected with our higher selves and not working towards a bigger vision, it is very easy to say yes to the wrong things. Saying yes, when you should say no, or doing things purely for the money could be the number one reason you feel drained and tired. It is an invisible battery drainer. Slowly, over time, we start to feel depleted as we are spending more time working on things that are not aligned with who we are and what we want.

So what is your purpose? Why do you do what you do? What do you want to accomplish? What do you want to leave to the world? Do you have a legacy?

Self-Love Step

I like to start with what I call the *"Perfect Day Exercise."* Take a notebook and a pen and write out your absolute *best*, most perfect day. Start from the minute you open your eyes.

Invoke the senses. What do you hear, smell, taste, and see?

So it might go a little like this, "I wake up in my bedroom; I can hear the waves crashing on the beach outside. I love looking around my bedroom. It is organized and really feels homey."

Write about showering, going for breakfast, exercising, and how you work. What do you do at work? How is your income delivered to you?

This exercise unlocks so many key insights into what you want your world to look like. When you know what your working day looks like, you can later start to plan out how you can create the income-producing activities to make it happen.

Vision & Legacy

If you could fast-forward five years, how does your business look? Do you employ people? Do you have a team working for you? What purpose does your business have? How does it help people? Reconnecting with our bigger vision can really alleviate a lot of angst and pressure. It will be the small things you do well on a daily basis that will contribute to your overall success. Having crystal clear clarity around your bigger vision is important, as it will enable you to start putting the pieces in place to accomplish the bigger mission!

Self-Love Step

In your notebook, now write out your bigger vision for your business, including who you serve and specifically how you help them. If you died tomorrow, what would you like to leave behind? How would you like to be remembered?

Mission & Message

So often we end up working *inside* our business and not *on* our business. It's easy to get so caught up making money, that we don't stop to realign and reconnect. Being aligned in your business is so important. Knowing your values and core beliefs, and not forsaking them, is critical. If you become disorientated in your business, you will start to feel run down and offtrack, wondering, "Am I even on the right path?"

We are always on the path we are meant to be on or we wouldn't be there. As Dolly Parton says, *"If you want the rainbow you gotta put up with the rain."*

When you can absolutely nail your message and what you stand for, you can start to craft the essence of your business. To truly capture your spirit and your essence, and put a "feel" to what you do, it's imperative you spend some time on your message and your mission.

You may feel everything I have shared up until now involves too much detail. You may just want the keys to an outrageously successful marketing plan. Well, sweetness, this is the key. It is the very start!

When a skyscraper is built, first the foundations must be laid and must be a strong enough foundation to support a skyscraper. This is what we are doing in these pages for your business. I have worked both for money and for love, and I can tell you first-hand that working within something you love is so much more rewarding than just working for the money.

When we start to build our brand, our message, and our business—particularly online—everything is visual. People can only make assumptions based on what they see from you. We have entered the age of connection marketing. People do not want to be sold to. We can influence a person's desire to buy from us by crafting a powerful, purpose-driven message.

With a strong message, people will want to follow you to the moon and back, and they will want to buy from you. If your marketing is structured with a strong foundation, the other "stuff" will start to fall into place.

Self-Love Step

Your values should become a part of your brand. What do you stand for or against? What gets you angry or makes you want to ride bare-back naked down a street for your cause? Now write out a list of your top five values. What is it you stand for? This will become a part of your larger mission.

Ignition

When it's time for take-off, we need to bring it all in and combine it to make it work together. A compelling personal, powerful, story and message is the starting point. This effectively helps you attract the *right* people, and those you actually love to work with. If you are a punk-rocker and you are "hard core," make this your brand and stay true to you. If you are spiritual and have strong spiritual beliefs, reflect this in your brand and message.

Your story, mission, and vision are the key things you will lay down to start growing a global, viral, passion brand. They add the "feel" to your online, otherwise "impersonal," world. When people feel like they know, like, and trust you, they will be more likely to buy from you. Begin to include your story, mission, and vision in the bio sections of all your social media.

When we look at growing your brand online, we start with the foundation, which is mapping out and getting clarity on your vision, mission, and purpose.

There are many tools for online connection. They are all used to increase your visibility, and all are designed so that you can give value to your potential clients before they even meet you. Following is a short list of tools you can use to connect authentically with others. Try not to be overwhelmed with this list, and also don't feel you have to master every single tool on the list. I normally suggest to my clients to pick one or two and learn the fundamentals of them first. Video, blogging, and Facebook will probably be the most effective for you. If what you do is visual, Pinterest may also be very powerful. Use any or all of them for the purpose of adding value, and to limit sales spiel (with exception of your blog or website).

Blog- This can be used as your website. It can look like a website, but rather than being somewhat static, it is designed to connect with your audience. This is the place where you share your wisdom. I use and recommend *Wordpress* for this purpose. It is incredibly powerful, and exceptionally simple to use. An added benefit is that *Google* loves *Wordpress* sites. Your blog should be at the heart of all your online activity. All your social media and online connection tools should send people back to your blog.

Youtube- Make video a part of your arsenal. It is the number one way you can start to build a connection with your audience. When making your first video, record it three times and don't watch any of them, just delete them and watch your fourth. You will feel so much more comfortable by the fourth video. Wondering what you should talk about? Talk about solutions to your client's problems. Learn what keeps them awake at night and figure out how you can help them, and then address that. Talk about your beliefs, your values, and how you can help them, without sounding like you are giving a sales pitch.

Facebook- Logging in to Facebook is the first thing most people do every day! It has honestly been the most effective marketing tool I have ever used. The main reason is that with Facebook advertising you can completely target and hone in on your market. Never before have we seen something this powerful. You could literally go from unknown to global in a very short space of time starting with Facebook alone.

However, be wary of putting all your eggs in one basket, since it's not smart to build your business to rely solely on something you don't own or of which you don't have full control. This is why your blog is your heart-space and central hub online.

Pinterest and *Twitter* are additional tools you can use to up the ante on the relationship-building funnel. They are also great tools to drive traffic to your website.

The most important thing you must do before you start using any of these traffic-driving tools is to put in place a way to build a database, so that when people land on your site or your Facebook page you have a way to convert them into a reader or buyer.

We are all so busy. It's easy to forget what websites we have gone to or who we have seen. If you can at least get someone signed up to stay connected to you, you have the opportunity to drip-feed your valuable info to them and get them back to your website.

If someone is online looking for a solution to a problem and they find you, but it's not easy for them to buy from you, they will keep looking until they have a solution to a problem. You owe it to them and to yourself to make sure you are structured in a way to capitalize on your website visitors.

Remember, if things aren't feeling quite right, then they probably aren't, and it's likely your internal navigation system is telling you to stop and recollect your thoughts. Go easy on yourself. Allow, breathe, and feel your way through it. Rome wasn't built in a day and neither will your business. Aim to stay in flow and in your truth, and the journey will be fun instead of frustrating, and you won't be wearing down your sanity or your health.

About Kat Mikic

Kat Mikic is passionate about helping women launch and grow a thriving online profile and business. She is the founder of *Women's Web Marketing* and has been using social media to grow and launch businesses since before most people even knew Facebook existed. Kat's mission is to help you become a woman of influence and the "go-to" person in your niche, so that you can create alternate income streams that are not reliant on you always having to be in your business.

Find out more about Kat Mikic on her website: WomensWebMarketing.com

♥

"Loving Yourself First" Note on Fear and Weakness

"If there exists no possibility of failure,
then victory is meaningless."

-Robert H. Schuller

Fear and weakness both have two sides, a negative side that can bring about great discouragement and render you powerless, and a positive side that can facilitate growth and healthy self-love.

As much as we hate to see fear or weakness show up, they each actually serve an important purpose. They are valuable gifts in disguise! Let's first address the seemingly big one, fear.

Once fear gets its grip on you, it can cause you to go downhill pretty fast, and once down, it can hold you there for a long time. That's because fear is the opposite of the power-pushers, *faith* and *love!*

Fear is the opposite of faith, because it is a lack of trust, including a lack of trust in yourself and your God-given abilities, a lack of trust in others, and a lack of trust in your Source (in God).

Fear is the opposite of love because it causes you to overly focus on yourself and magnify your limits, which are selfish and controlling acts! When you are busy focusing on what's wrong with you, guess what? You cannot be there in an appropriate way for yourself or for others.

That's right! Fear is about you believing that *you* have to have all the answers. It is *you* trying to be in control! *Always* being in control keeps you from looking above for inspiration and direction. *Always* being in control takes energy from your heart and mind as well, which leaves you depleted and unlikely to be filled up with love.

Fear brings with it some gifts! Fear's opposite, faith, is one of those gifts. Faith causes you to rise up and look beyond the fear, and to say something strong, mighty, and powerful right smack dab in the middle of your negative emotions. It then transports you to new heights, new views, and new and better outcomes.

Even in business (yes, where you may make lots of money), faith and belief are ways of letting go of control and trusting the supernatural source of all abundance.

Fear is common to us all, and is only a problem if we choose to let it linger and not teach us. The fear that crops up in your life holds a hidden desire (another valuable gift) at its very root, and that desire is almost always something pure and good, so focus on that desire (that gift) instead of the fear.

Here is a great way to think of it. Your fear is an ugly package that holds within it something very beautiful you have been longing for. The gift-wrapping is so hideous that if you were not being aware, you would quickly throw the whole package out. Instead, you know to tear off the ugly wrapping to reveal the most wonderful gift you can imagine, a gift that helps you fully empower yourself!

For example, if your fear is that you think you cannot pay your bills, then your true desire (the gift) may be that you want to provide a good lifestyle for yourself and your family. If your fear is that you will not have customers, your pure desire (the gift) may be that you want to serve others, offering great benefits and value in exchange for a financial benefit for you, so that everyone wins! Focus on the positive desire, which is the exceptional gift hidden within the fear-wrapped package!

Now, what about weakness? I think you will be encouraged to know, that we all have areas of weakness too, and that every weakness also comes with a precious and valuable gift!

The gift is that without weakness, we would not witness the strength of something much bigger and much greater with us and within us! The power and strength of the divine working on your behalf shows up almost exclusively in your point of weakness. Without weakness, you would never see this miracle power!

Jane North Lyon, the Writer of Chapter 6

Jane North Lyon is someone I am deeply honored and incredibly blessed to know. She was my college roommate at Texas A&M University for several wonderful years starting in 1981. Back then, I was a bit of a tomboy fresh out of Long Island, NY, with a street-smart attitude and a Yankee accent as thick as a Texas steak! Jane was polite, proper, and well-composed, with a heart full of love, a warm, one-of-a-kind laugh, and an adorable sense of humor that made me like her right from the start!

In a sense, Jane was like a big-sister, mom-figure, and fun girlfriend all rolled into one. From the day we met she always had my back and my best interests in mind. I learned so much from her about generosity, kindness, God, the world, lambskins, studying, improving my grammar and manners, cooking duck, and the value of people and friends.

Jane and I have stayed in contact for over 30 years and have cheered each other on as we got married, moved to different cities, had lots of babies (who grew into marvelous grown-up people), lost dear and precious friends, and started and grew our businesses, and I can say without reservation and without any hesitation whatsoever that Jane North Lyon is a woman of tremendously high integrity, and she has remained constant and steadfast throughout these many years! I can't say that about too many people, but I easily say it about Jane. Anyone who knows her would say the same thing!

There is something amazingly powerful about making a positive impact on others, and influencing lives for the better by the way you live your life, without even realizing you are doing it. That's exactly what Jane does. More people should live this way.

Margo DeGange

♥

Chapter 6
Growing Things Change: Fear into Victory and Weakness into Strength

By Jane North Lyon, Educator for Award-Winning
Curricula in Pre-School Music & Movement,
and Children's World Drumming

Clammy hands gripping the steering wheel, stomach churning, my list of pre-schools . . . potential clients . . . sitting beside me there in my red minivan, my route highlighted on a map. I swore I'd never be in sales, yet here I was doing "cold calls" to grow the new business I had started. It was that same queasy feeling of being the new kid in seventh grade, and awkwardly carrying my lunch tray up and down each row of tables, scanning for friendly and inviting faces, and fearing there were none.

This Time, It's Personal

I had never experienced anxiety when dropping in on business owners before, when I was representing the PTA or band boosters, asking for donations or other support. So, this fear was new to me, and I wondered why. I discovered, after some analysis, that it was because this time it was personal. I didn't have a concern asking for a business owner's support on behalf of a school organization, because if they weren't interested, their disinterest or rejection was not aimed at me. In this situation, however, I took it as a personal defeat if they didn't jump up from their desk and shout, "Hallelujah, we've been looking for someone to teach music at our pre-school!"

Now, I was vulnerable, because I was "selling" myself, my talents, my confidence, my abilities, my personality, my qualifications. If a pre-school director seemed minimally interested when I dropped by on a "cold call," I received it as disdain toward me, personally.

Pursuing a Passion

Twenty years earlier, I had earned my Bachelor of Science in Agriculture Journalism from a major university, and worked as a newspaper photographer and editor for about six years before starting a family with my husband. I stayed home for the next 16 years, making a little extra here and there doing newsletters and brochures for non-profits, and also doing wedding photography. When our fourth child was about to start kindergarten, we knew I needed to return to work because we were weary of pinching pennies. We also knew that college tuition was in the not-too-distant future, but returning to the newspaper world was not at all appealing in this season of my life. So, I had a talk with God. I remember it basically word-for-word. "God, You know my heart's desire is to have my own business, to make my own decisions. You know I don't mind working hard . . . I've been working hard for free a number of years as PTA president, room mom, and fund-raising vice president, but I want to 'work smart.' Please help me find the right business that will fill me with energy and passion, not drain me of it."

Not too long after that, we took a family road trip from Texas to South Carolina to visit some very close friends who had moved there a couple of years earlier. Richard and my husband, Brent, are close friends; Richard's wife, Cristi, and I are close friends; and our kids had all grown up in church nursery together. Before our friends moved away, Richard had been our church worship minister and children's minister for years, and Brent (on the guitar) and I (as a vocalist) had been on the worship team with him for quite some time. In South Carolina, Richard had become a licensee for an award-winning music and movement curriculum, and invited me to join him for his morning of classes at one of the pre-schools where he taught. After participating with him in the classes, I asked him, "Richard, do you think I could start a business like this back in Texas?" He replied, "You *so* could! I wish you lived here, 'cause I'd hire you!"

I have loved singing ever since I was a young child. My parents always teased me that I was singing before I could talk. I sang in middle school, high school, and college choirs; then worship groups at church; and sang a lot with my children– while rocking them to sleep, or as a way of distracting them from whatever had upset them, or marching around the room together when listening to a "Goliath" song, and then even singing hymns to one of my teenagers who asked me to do so each night while rubbing her back at bedtime. I had no idea that the music activities I did with my children, out of a natural desire to engage with them musically and respond together to music, was actually part of a research-based philosophy of music-learning.

It took me one year to ruminate on the possibility of starting this business teaching pre-school music at child development centers. My husband encouraged me to develop a business plan and a goal for growth, because our finances needed a "real" business, not a hobby like previous endeavors.

My first pre-school client was owned by a family friend, and I stayed in the "one-client zone" for my first year in business, to "get my feet wet" learning the curriculum, researching and educating myself in music and movement philosophies, and weaning myself from having been a professional volunteer at my kids' schools.

As our pastor had said, "growing things change." A seed cannot become a plant that supplies hundreds more seeds until it submits to the change that growth requires. As my husband said, "Being satisfied with the status quo is the beginning of the end for a business." I am so thankful for wise men in my life!

Self-Talk

Do you ever "self-talk"? King David did a lot of "self-talking." "Why are you in despair, my soul? Why are you disturbed within me? Hope in God, because I will praise Him once again, since His presence saves me and He is my God" (Psalm 43:5). "Bless the Lord, O my soul: and all that is within me, bless His holy name. Bless the LORD, O my soul, and forget not all His benefits: Who forgives all your iniquities; Who heals all your diseases; Who redeems your life from destruction; Who crowns you with loving kindness and tender mercies; Who satisfies your mouth with good things; so that your youth is renewed like the eagle's" (Psalm 103:1-5).

I have to self-talk, and oftentimes I must ask myself out loud, "What is the priority for today?" The answer might be as basic as, "Be on time to work." I might then leave the dishes or unanswered e-mails for another time during the day, so that I can accomplish the priority of simply being on time.

So, as my clammy hands grip the steering wheel, ready to venture out on "cold calls" to area pre-schools, I am self-talking *and* praying. My self-talk consists of acknowledging that if I don't take this great idea and make something of it, then someone else will. One reason my hands are gripping the steering wheel so tightly is to be sure I don't just take the next U-turn, find something chocolate and gooey to eat, and just go home. I have to purpose in my mind that I cannot go home defeated, having not even tried, and that the only person with the power to defeat me is . . . me. "What are you afraid of?" I ask myself. "No one is going to physically hurt you." Still, rejection does hurt. Anyone who has been bitten by that vicious vixen carries the scars, and perhaps the still-festering wounds.

So, my self-talk then progresses to prayer. There is only so much that can be accomplished in this natural realm. I cannot self-talk myself into conjuring up a change in my nature. I must place my confidence and trust in the One who loves me, the One who says I am more than a conqueror, who says He is with me always.

I quite literally pray myself all the way into the next pre-school parking lot. "Lord, I consider myself a strong person, and other people have told me they view me as a strong person; but in this area I am weak. You say that in my weaknesses, You are made strong. I need Your strength. I need You to be strong through me. This kind of thing does not come naturally to me, and it's completely out of my comfort zone, but You are my comfort, You are my ability, You are my strength. I pray that You would go ahead of me, and provide me with the right person to talk to, and they would take my materials to the decision-makers, and that You would give me favor . . . not because I deserve it, but because I have placed my faith in You, and Your Word says that through faith righteousness is imputed to me, and also that the steps of the righteous are ordered of the Lord. Proverbs 16:3 says that when I roll my works upon You and commit them wholly to You, that You will cause my thoughts to become agreeable to Your will, and so shall my plans be established and succeed."

Fear into Victory; Weakness into Strength

I would love to write that, "Boom!" I prayed and immediately overcame the fear and anxiety, but it was a process, and it took years. There were occasions when I would go out on a "cold call" and feel so awful afterward that I would not attempt to reach out to a new pre-school for about three months. It wasn't that I had been treated poorly; it's just that the whole process was not my natural bent. I could teach music to children and sing and march and drum with them for most of the day, and be quite happy with that, but in order to get to that place of interacting with the children, first I had to do what was so very unnatural for me, and quite distasteful, at that, which was dropping in on the schools, uninvited.

As with most challenges, the result has to either be failure and defeat, or success and victory.

I am happy to say that the thing that once brought me close to nausea, is now something I can do as a natural expression of my passion for what I do. What was once my weakness is now my strength, but it would have never been so if I had made excuses for myself and not submitted to the growth process.

Growing Things Change: The Stages

The Seed Stage- For every growth stage in a plant or in a person, there has to be a beginning. The seed stage can be the most difficult for someone starting a business. There is amazing potential, and there are great ideas, but how do we start? Like a seed planted in the soil, sometimes we have to be in a dark, smelly, gritty place and push through it in order to grow. This is the stage where we have to identify our weaknesses. Then we have to purposefully overcome those weaknesses, not making excuses for why we have those weaknesses, or who is at fault for them.

The Growth Stage- As weaknesses are overcome, then growth can occur in one's character as well as in one's business. However, just like a plant that is growing quickly, pruning must take place if there is to be any fruit. My apple tree sprouts many new branches each spring. Still, I have to prune the small branches away, in order for the nutrients to be supplied to the branches which are established enough to bear the weight of the apples that will grow on them. When I see a huge bunch of apples growing in one area, I have to pick off and throw away some of them in each grouping, or they will all wind up small and undeveloped. We have to identify the things in our businesses that are taking up too much time and effort, and that create stress, without results; and prune them away. Then our energies and creativity can flow generously to the areas of our business that have the potential to be most fruitful.

The Fruit-Bearing Stage- "Slow and steady wins the race," as the saying goes. Businesses that experience fast and furious growth oftentimes do not have the infrastructure and financial stability to handle that pace of growth, and then the businesses crash and burn. If the previous stages of overcoming weaknesses (Seed Stage) and pruning away unnecessary time-suckers and energy-suckers (Growth Stage) have been accomplished, then the fruit-bearing can begin. If I let my tomato plants grow wildly outside their tomato cages, I have quite impressively-large tomato plants, but very little fruit. If I have been faithful to prune them back during the Growth Stage, snipping away languishing branches or an excess of new branches, then I have prepared the plant to produce a bumper crop.

The Sharing Stage- This is the stage of growth that is often overlooked. One of my favorite things about vegetable gardening and harvesting my apples is sharing the abundance with others. It's an absolute delight to bring a large bag of apples to my good friend's mother, who loves to make apple butter. In business, we need to remember that it was people who helped bring us to The Fruit-Bearing Stage, and therefore we need to look for ways to give back. Giving back does not necessarily have to be toward the ones who mentored us, encouraged us, gave us opportunities, or shared networking contacts. If I have helped someone, in some way, to develop and grow their business, encouraged them around concerns they had in parenting, or shared with them truths for their divisive relationships, I don't need them to necessarily return the favor. Instead, it's far more delightful to watch them invest in, mentor, or encourage someone else. My husband and I have several "parenting anthems"—convictions that have been a framework for raising our children, and one of those anthems is admonishing our children to be givers, not takers.

Becoming a purposeful giver is really not hard, and this is what it might look like: letting the person behind you in the grocery store check-out line go ahead of you, because they have just a few items; tipping a waitress well; calling a store manager to tell them the name of one of their associates who gave you outstanding service; buying another box of cookie dough from the student who comes to your door, raising funds for their PTA, when you just bought a box the day before; paying for someone's burger or coffee when you are ahead of them in a drive-through; opening your home as a place for your teenagers' friends to come hang out, even if it's dirty and cluttered; or making a meal for someone who just had a baby, or has a family member in the hospital.

The possibilities are endless, but first we must be awake and aware, so we can see a need when it presents itself. In my business, I do not charge pre-school music tuition for the children of the staff members at the school. I am acutely aware that I am a guest in the school, so that is one of the ways I find to "return the blessing."

Self-Love Steps

1. Realize, accept, and own the fact that, for personal and business growth, you will have to change. This change could be in your natural "bent," the way you view yourself or others, or in your modus operandi (the habitual way you do things).

2. Self-talk. Speak out loud concerning the areas of your life that you know are your weaknesses, and ask God and other people for their help in how to overcome these weaknesses. This requires laying down our pride. Sometimes, it can be beneficial to ask others what they perceive are your weaknesses or natural personality bents that might inhibit personal or business growth. Oftentimes, we are the last ones to realize our own weaknesses—like negativity, always being right, inflexibility, etc.

3. Prune away the activities that are sapping your strength and passion, which are requiring too much attention and inhibiting personal and business growth.

4. Become a giver. You can pat yourself on the back for the strides you have taken in your personal and business life, but also be sure to understand and acknowledge the effect that others have had on you. Without the support and encouragement of our families, mentors, associates, and clients, we could not be in a place of growth. When I got a new client early in my business, my eight year-old daughter got a marker and wrote on a piece of paper, "Good job, Mommy! I'm proud of you!" I taped that note up in my kitchen, and it has remained there for eight years, and encourages me still to this day. Her act of giving in that moment had a profound effect on me. Do not be afraid to give to complete strangers, or those who you don't believe "deserve" your help. You will be surprised at what an incredible investment this can be in others as well as yourself.

One of the most lucrative pay-offs to being in business for ourselves is the opportunity that is presented to each of us for personal growth as people of compassion, integrity, and creativity. As we change through the growth process, we have the ability—and also the power—to affect change in other people's lives, in addition to our own.

Fear or victory; weakness or strength? I know what I choose. I choose to grow.

About Jane North Lyon

Jane North Lyon, a graduate of Texas A&M University, spent several years as a newspaper photographer, reporter, and editor. After promoting to motherhood, she raised her four children at home and in 2004, started a business teaching an award-winning pre-school music and movement curriculum, then expanded it as an authorized retailer for *Folkmanis®* puppets and quality children's percussion instruments. A small teaching staff assists her. She and her husband, Brent—married over 30 years—reside near Fort Worth, Texas.

Find out more about Jane North Lyon on her website: MissJane.MusicTeachersHelper.com

♥

"Loving Yourself First" Note on Social Media Simplicity

"Distracted from distraction by distraction."

-T.S. Eliot

It's easy to neglect self-love when it comes to social media: Facebook, Twitter, LinkedIn, Pinterest, Flickr, Foursquare . . . feel overwhelmed yet? If not, we don't have to stop there, since there are thousands more social media sites to know about and experience. It tires me out to think about it!

Just because something exists online does not mean you have to access it, be involved with it, or engage in it the way everyone else does, and just because some "expert" or someone important says you must "be all over" social media for the sake of your business, does not mean you should necessarily follow their lead. There are a lot of people saying a lot of things about social media. Many of them are just guessing and stressing! When I consider the immense pressure all around us to haphazardly plug into social media for both personal and professional reasons, I often wonder where our common sense has gone.

So many people are online without a purpose or plan. It could be that we are a little too social when, for the sake of our well-being, at times we should happily disengage, withdraw, reflect, and unwind. This is especially true when we find ourselves neglecting our face-to-face relationships because we are overly buried online.

Lifestyle Design is about quality of life. It includes creating fabulous businesses that serve us well and provide for our needs and beyond. It also includes fashioning lives that are meaningful, purposeful, and nourishing to the soul. We can do that when we are balanced, and when we draw the necessary boundary lines that keep one area of our life or business from taking over the rest. Everything must have its fitting time and place.

Social media is a fabulous tool for reaching the world and connecting with the people you want to know and with those you want to reach, but it is a tool, not a lifestyle. Think about it this way: before social media existed, you were not likely on the phone, at a party, at the coffee shop, or in a conversation 24/7. In your business, you did not run non-stop, consistent, and consecutive radio, magazine, and T.V. ads, or stop to talk business with every single person on the strip! It is highly unlikely that in your pre-social media life, you neglected family, friends, hobbies, relationships, recreation, music, exercise, and bubble baths in exchange for constant chatter with people you barely knew.

It sounds crazy when you think of it like that, but in a sense that's what many of us do with social media. We overdo it in time and effort, and under-do it in terms of planning and results. We over-engage with no clear purpose, and we often exchange important chunks of our life for a shot-in-the-dark approach to success. Then, when we are left exhausted and depleted from too much activity and no measurable and beneficial results, we get discouraged and blame ourselves for not doing it "right," or for not being as good in business or at connecting with people as the other gal or guy!

Social media tools are so prevalent, so great in number, and so easily accessed that if you don't want them to become a burden and overtake your work and life, you *must* approach them with a well-designed plan. A plan that is simple yet powerful.

Love yourself first by reflecting on why and how you use social media, and make the necessary changes to be more effective, and also to live more fully. If any activity in your life or business feels like a tremendous burden, then it *is* a burden! If it robs you of joy, takes away from the relationships and the activities that mean the most to you, and brings few positive results, then you really should question why or how you do that particular thing!

Rick Cooper, the Writer of Chapter 7

I actually met Rick Cooper through social media, and his presence there struck a chord with me. I saw early on that all of his communications were warm, appealing, and true to his brand. His message was consistent and clear, and I could easily and clearly see that his mission in business was to help others make significant and meaningful connections online. Right off the bat I sensed he was a man of integrity, and I saw how that showed up in his business and in his leadership. I liked what I saw of him online.

Eventually, Rick reached out to me for a phone conversation, and we actually had more than one. I liked him even more when I spoke with him by phone, because I heard the sincerity in his voice and the warmth in his tone. It was easy to talk to him. He is polite, respectful, knowledgeable, and fun to chat with.

I will say that all of our communications have been very positive, with a definite sense of purpose. What I know about Rick is that he truly wants to help business owners grow and

prosper, and he wants them to enjoy their lives, a families, too. He is definitely a balanced guy!

Rick and I have a number of mutual colleagues. particular, who is a terrific person and a very distin woman in her field, and who knows Rick personally a told me what a wonderful and genuine person she saw be. She said his knowledge of social media and relation what makes him a true expert in the field. She went on t that Rick truly cares about helping people build a p platform for social media, and that anyone who worl Rick will automatically know they are in good ha completely and totally agree!

Margo DeGange

prosper, and he wants them to enjoy their lives, and their families, too. He is definitely a balanced guy!

Rick and I have a number of mutual colleagues. One in particular, who is a terrific person and a very distinguished woman in her field, and who knows Rick personally and well, told me what a wonderful and genuine person she saw Rick to be. She said his knowledge of social media and relationships is what makes him a true expert in the field. She went on to share that Rick truly cares about helping people build a positive platform for social media, and that anyone who works with Rick will automatically know they are in good hands. I completely and totally agree!

Margo DeGange

♥

Chapter 7
Social Media Simplicity
for Ease of Use and Peace of Mind

By Rick Cooper, MBA, Online Marketing
and Social Media Expert

Social media gives you the capability to find new clients and grow your business. Every day, entrepreneurs visit Facebook, Twitter, and LinkedIn to connect with people and develop new relationships. Social media gives you a quick and easy way to stay in touch and follow up. It is easy to use if you remember a few simple rules.

Social media can also be a source of stress. If you want to leverage this powerful resource while maintaining your peace of mind, then implement the strategies below.

Focus on Developing Relationships

"Ask yourself this question CONSTANTLY: where can I add the most value to what matters most to me and the people who care about me?" -Chris Brogan

There are two ways to communicate with people through social media. You can communicate with people one-on-one, or you can share a message with your network. While it is beneficial to reach a lot of people at once, there is high value in building relationships one at a time.

I have met a lot of great people through social media. Michele Jennae is Founder of influenSPHERE, a company dedicated to helping people strategically expand their sphere of influence. I first met Michele through Twitter and began to retweet her inspirational messages. She did the same for me, retweeting my messages and including my Twitter ID @RickCooper (I share other people's content as a way to deliver value to my followers and build social currency). After that, we became friends on Facebook. People tend to share more personal information on Facebook, and that makes it easier to learn more about them. We both live in Sacramento but we had never met in person even though we both attend local networking events.

Michele invited me to be a guest on her BlogTalkRadio show. I shared ideas on networking strategies and social media. We finally had an opportunity to meet through a local group called the *Sacramento Speakers Network*. It was nice to finally meet in person.

Social media is a powerful tool for communication. You can meet people, develop relationships, and do business together. However, there will always be a benefit in meeting people in person.

"You can be professional while also "keeping it real" with your customers. By interacting with customers in a less formal way, you'll build a strong human connection that helps build brand loyalty." -David Hauser

Let Go of the Need to Respond to Everything Happening Online

One of the challenges business owners have with social media is that they feel the need to respond to everything people post. This is just not possible.

Your news feed is full of posts. Whether on Facebook, Twitter or LinkedIn, new content is always being shared. You don't have to respond to everything. Be selective.

Keep Your Interactions Positive and Supportive

The relationships you develop on social media can be beneficial and enjoyable, but realize that you are probably connected to a lot of people you don't know well, and who you probably wouldn't be friends with in real life. Don't feel compelled to keep anyone as a friend on social media if the relationship does not support you. When people have an issue, they often turn to social media, and in particular Facebook, to share it.

Some people thrive on drama. They love to share bad news and get into arguments. Here are five tips to keep your interactions positive on social media:

1. Avoid conflict.

2. Don't air your dirty laundry on social media.

3. Filter out posts from people who are negative.

4. Delete negative comments from your Facebook page.

5. Remove people from your network who aren't a good fit.

People tend to feed off of negative energy. If you post a negative message, you will attract people who want to argue, and that will start a negative downward spiral. Keep your messages positive and optimistic.

Protect your privacy. Big data is watching. Whatever you post is archived and available to the government, organizations and others.

Set Boundaries

Is it possible to be too connected? Is it harmful to spend too much time on social media? I think the answer is yes. The random nature of posts in your news feed can be very overwhelming.

From time to time, you need to disconnect from social media and have some alone time or visit with friends in person. This can be very relaxing and liberating. Take a walk, meditate, and pray. Don't let what others post affect how you feel. Don't let it change your attitude from positive to negative.

Have a Social Media Plan

"Monitor, engage, and be transparent; these have always been the keys to success in the digital space."
-Dallas Lawrence

Do you have a social media plan? You will benefit from taking action to achieve your desired outcomes. Here are five quick tips to increase your effectiveness on social media:

1. Set social media goals.

2. Identify your most important activities.

3. Develop a daily routine.

4. Post messages with links to your blog, online videos, and lead capture pages.

5. Apply the 80/20 rule to social media

More on Applying the 80/20 Rule to Social Media

You can apply the 80/20 rule to social media. 80 percent of your posts should be informational and only 20 percent of your posts should be promotional. Informational posts include tips, strategies, techniques, questions, and personal messages. Blog posts and videos are also informational. Promotional posts include sharing lead capture pages, event invitations, and special promotions.

Social media is social. Communicating on Facebook is like going to a networking event. It's a great place to meet people, have conversations and develop relationships.

Don't try to force things to happen. Let go of the outcome. Have a plan, select strategies, and implement them. Then, step back and let it work. I use Facebook ads to promote events and get more likes on my Facebook Page. When you try to force things, it can turn people off. Instead, focus on adding value. Think about what other people are interested in, and talk about it.

I'm passionate about helping small business owners leverage technology to grow their businesses online. I started my business back in 2003. I worked in the corporate world for over a dozen years. I loved what I was doing but I felt something was missing. When I was back in college, I had the opportunity to become President of an organization on campus called *The Entrepreneurial Network*. We brought in local business owners to share their story with students. It lit a fire inside me that inspired me to one day start my own business.

In the Fall of 2001, we all witnessed a life-changing event. September 11th changed the way we looked at life. And it got me re-focused on my vision of starting my own business. That opportunity came to pass in May 2003. And I've been helping business owners ever since.

When I founded my company, MySpace was the most popular social media site. LinkedIn was just getting started. Back then, I saw the potential of social media. But it took a long time to get results. Many of the benefits of social media come only after you build a large network.

What are you doing to build your network? Take consistent action, but don't be too aggressive. Many social networks will penalize you if you try to add too many friends too quickly. Facebook will suspend your ability to add friends for a period of time if you try to add friends too quickly.

Automate Social Media While Remaining Authentic

Have you ever had a time when you wanted to post something on Facebook, but didn't know what to say? It's hard to be spontaneously brilliant in the moment. There is an easier way. You can create a content library with messages you write when you are feeling creative.

You can save time and effort by automating social media. You can post messages consistently using a free service like Hootsuite.

Does that mean that you don't interact live with people online? Not at all! Share personal updates and be authentic. Respond back to people. Scheduling future posts will free you up to become more active in Facebook groups and LinkedIn groups.

Be a Rapid Responder

"Engaging in an authentic, meaningful conversation with consumers will be the key to marketing success and growth, even if that means acknowledging negative feedback; transparency is paramount." -Ron Blake

Imagine going to a networking event. Someone asks you a question and then you stand there for five minutes in silence before answering the question. That would be rude, wouldn't it? And yet, people do this on social media all the time. People often ignore messages or wait days to respond back.

Develop the habit of being a rapid responder. When people send you a message or comment on your post, respond back quickly.

Help Others

There are people in your life who need a helping hand. From time to time, people need advice or an encouraging word. Who needs your help? What help do they need?

A great way to communicate with a friend on social media is to send a private message to say hello. This is an easy way to reach out and connect personally. When you send a message, keep it brief and end with a question. This will encourage them to reply back to you.

Social media gives you an amazing window into the lives of other people. Take this opportunity to help others and give back.

From time to time, I share a spiritual message with my network. I find a scriptural verse that I feel offers an inspiring message and then post it on Facebook. This is my way of sharing the good news!

Build Social Currency

Social currency is a simple way to earn goodwill by helping others out publicly on social media. Congratulate someone, acknowledge them, share an endorsement, or give a testimonial.

One day I was teaching a webinar on Facebook Marketing. I decided to demonstrate social currency by posting a message about an upcoming event held by International Speaker and celebrity Adryenn Ashley. I posted a message on my Facebook page. Within a few minutes, Adryenn commented on my post, thanking me for sharing her event.

I posted a comment asking if she wanted me to share her event in my e-mail newsletter. She said yes. Later that week, I sent her the newsletter. My newsletter includes my bio which mentions that I have worked as Affiliate Manager for Loral Langemeier and Eric Lofholm. Adryenn replied back and asked me if I wanted to be her Affiliate Manager for the upcoming event. I said yes and she hired me. That opportunity came to me because I was proactive in building social currency.

You have probably heard about the butterfly effect. A butterfly flapping its wings in Beijing could affect the weather thousands of miles away a few days later. It's a powerful concept. If you drop a stone in a still pond, it will create a ripple that expands out from the center. Wave after wave will spread out. Everything you do has an impact, sometimes large and sometimes small. Use social media for good. Focus on adding value and helping others. It will all come back to you in amazing ways!

Social media gives you a great opportunity to develop relationships. It's easy to take action daily, but it takes a commitment. I encourage you to make social media a priority.

One day in the near future, you may receive an amazing opportunity simply by communicating and adding value.

Self-Love Steps

1. Make a list of people you want to know better. That includes potential clients, joint venture partners and other influential people.

2. Contact five people personally through social media every day. It's worth the effort. I have met a lot of great people through social media.

About Rick Cooper

Rick Cooper is an online marketing and social media trainer. He works with small business owners who want to generate leads and earn sales online. He specializes in helping entrepreneurs leverage their expertise to attract clients. Rick is founder of *Social Media Outcomes*, based in Sacramento, California and author of *Seize Your Opportunities, Marketing Magic,* and *Extreme Excellence.* Rick is an international speaker and was featured in *Comstocks Magazine* and interviewed by *The National Networker.*

Find out more about Rick Cooper on his website: SocialMediaOutcomes.com

♥

"Loving Yourself First" Note on Building a Team

"Teamwork is so important that it is virtually impossible for you to reach the heights of your capabilities or make the money that you want without becoming very good at it."

-Brian Tracy

We've heard a million times that Rome wasn't built it a day, but we aren't reminded often enough that Rome wasn't built without the work of a team, either.

The one aspect of entrepreneurship that wears good people down fast is when they try to do it all themselves. Smart business owners get stuck in this trap every day. It begins when funds are low and we can't seem to afford to get the help we need. There is no extra money for such a "luxury," so we do it all ourselves. Months or years later, we may find that we have not advanced, we have not increased significantly in sales, we have not made things easier on ourselves, and we have not grown our profits because we are still in the trap.

Building a team is possible for every business owner, but it takes a leader's eye to both see the need for delegation, and to spot the opportunities that will help us to begin. Once you release a single business limb from the trap, you have more power to escape it completely, and that should be your goal. Always look for ways to delegate every activity in your business that does not absolutely require you to personally do it.

As the business owner, your objective should be to use your time only for activities that directly bring in money or that cause business growth, and activities that someone else just cannot do.

Let's say you are a speaker, and your company makes money from your events because people pay to hear what you have to say. Then, it makes total sense that you should invest your time doing as much speaking as you can, and leave things like ordering your marketing materials such as postcards and banners; formatting and sending your e-mail invitations; creating sign-up forms; interacting with meeting planners and hotel staff; and event set-up, to someone else.

Focus your energies on what you do well to increase profits and grow your business, and delegate the rest. You will likely create greater success—and much more quickly—with a team than without, and you will actually feel much less worn down, too!

Getting into a pattern of delegating, and building a team, takes time and money, but you start in small ways. Begin little by little to free up your time and get the infrastructure set up. Perhaps at first you could get the help of a college student for simple tasks, contracting them for just a few hours each month to do your newsletters. Or maybe you can trade-out services with a virtual assistant. Instead of doing your own book-keeping once a month, you could hire a book-keeper, and schedule an additional speaking gig during the month to pay for it. You must think in terms of growth. What can you do today to build your team and increase sales because of it? That is how a leader thinks!

Building a team is part of being a leader. You can expand your vision, and reach more people, when you are doing what you are passionate about and highly skilled at. Leave the other tasks to your team. This will keep you from feeling depleted and defeated. Instead, you will feel yourself serving from a position of true influence and strength.

Amanda Sue Howell, the Writer of Chapter 8

Amanda Sue Howell, is genuine and charming, with a quirky sense of humor that clearly shows her creative side. She is a wife and mom with a vision and a mission behind all that she does. This is a gal who knows how to stay positive, while working steadily towards her dreams, even with an enormous portion of responsibility on her plate. Through her many skills and talents, she is determined to grow her business to help not only herself and her family, but many people beyond her immediate circle.

Amanda believes strongly that we should grow as entrepreneurs so we can provide resources and opportunities for others. She "gets" that a team must be in place to support this growth as well as to help carry it out. Amanda's long-term goals include helping to repair orphanages in China, and setting up a foundation for women who've been through domestic violence. She knows it takes a team to make this happen.

I love Amanda's practical way of inspiring business owners to make the changes needed for success. She often uses everyday scenarios as examples we can all relate to. She wants *you* to "get it" too, and build your team, not so you can heap a bunch of treasures on yourself, but so you can create a meaningful life, and leave to the world a legacy of kindness, helpfulness, and purpose.

Margo DeGange

♥

Chapter 8
Build Yourself Up
by Building Yourself a Team

By Amanda Sue Howell, The Coach for Quirky Creativest

- Diplomats
- Presidents
- Kings & queens
- Spiritual leaders

What do they all have in common? Teams! Diplomats have entourages. The President of the United States has the Cabinet. The Queen of England has Parliament. Jesus had His apostles. None of them were out there alone.

I used to be one of those people who wanted to be left alone. I thought it was easier to work with no distractions. Then one day, a friend asked me to help her out for an afternoon. She was working in an assisted living facility. I don't recall the entire scenario, but for some reason they were short-staffed that day.

As it turned out, one of the major duties she had was laundry. At the time, laundry was one of my most hated chores. But you've gotta do, what you've gotta do, so we set to work. We were in there for hours folding sheets and towels, but while we were working, we talked about upcoming events (we were both in a music ministry), and recent movies we'd seen, and whatever came to mind.

You know what happened? Not only did one of my least favorite chores suddenly become a lot more enjoyable, but the time flew by so fast! When she looked at her watch and figured out her shift was up, it shocked me. I had expected the day to really drag on and on. Our teamwork made the task more pleasant, and we got a lot more done in that timeframe than either of us could have done alone.

So how does this affect you and your business? What makes teams so valuable to an entrepreneur? Let me share five reasons why it's so vital to have a team for your business, and then I'll go into further detail. I'll also give action steps ("Self-Love Steps") so you can start moving in the right direction. Don't worry; I work in a scary-free zone, so all of the Self-Love Steps will be super easy.

Don't be concerned much if your business isn't ready for teams. We are all in different stages. If you've just started your business, you might not need a team just yet. If you're a bit further in your business growth, you may be starting to plan for a team. Or you might be advanced, and already formulating your team. Regardless of where you are in your business, I hope you find this lesson encouraging and informative.

Five Reasons Why Building a Business Team Is Important:

1. It releases you to do the work you're best at doing.

2. It's the responsible thing for a business owner to do.

3. It's important for the health of your business.

4. It's important for the health of your relationships.

5. It's important for *your* health.

It Releases You to Do the Work You're Meant to Do

This is one of my major frustrations with a lot of business owners, so forgive me if I step on the soapbox for a moment. Many entrepreneurs are under the impression that they should be doing everything in their business. I don't know if they're afraid it won't really be *their* business, or if experience has convinced them that things won't be done properly unless they do it.

Let me put this as simply as possible. No one is good at everything. You may be good at a lot of things, but you're not good at everything. Additionally, being good at something doesn't mean you enjoy doing it. And you should enjoy your work!

Here is an example. I'm a smart woman. I'm not bragging, just letting you know, so you know where I'm coming from. I can do coding. What I don't know about coding, I could learn. But I can't stand coding. I have friends who find coding to be truly enjoyable. On the flip side, they don't like doing crafts, but I love crafts.

Here's another example. I am technically able to do copywriting. I have done my own copywriting. I don't enjoy it at all. I do just fine, and I get great feedback on it, but it makes me want to smash my head against the keyboard. I have a friend who has literally written such amazing copy, that one of her clients wept for joy when she read her new site copy. The only one who cries over my copy is me. And those aren't tears of joy, that's pure frustration, baby!

Okay so I don't really cry, but you get my point. When you have a team to handle the things you don't enjoy doing, you are free to spend time doing the work you're really good at, and odds are it'll be the stuff you prefer doing anyway.

Food for thought:

Your team can appear in many forms. It can include a virtual assistant (like an administrative assistant, but someone who is a contract worker), a bookkeeper, and a copy writer. Hiring the right members shouldn't feel scary at all. Really amazing teams feel more like a small family than just office staff. (Laura Roeder's team, and Photojojo.com's team are great examples.)

Self-Love Step

Start thinking of work you don't like doing, and imagine what your business day will look like when you no longer have to handle that yourself. Write those thoughts down on paper.

It's the Responsible Thing for a Business Owner to Do

I believe that we have a responsibility as business owners to provide jobs. Not just to boost the economy, but to provide open doors and opportunities to people who need them.

Self-Love Step

Open your heart to the idea of having a team. Once your heart is open to the idea, your mind will start noticing possibilities for future teammates.

Having a quality team opens your business to growth, which leads me to my next point of why building a team is important.

It's Important for the Health of Your Business

"So, whether you eat or drink, or whatever you do, do all to the glory of God" (1Corinthians 10:3).

If we are doing all things to the glory of God, we are doing all things excellently. A business that is run with excellence can't help but to prosper and grow.

Expansion comes in all different forms. Sometimes it means opening up another branch. If you're a service-based business, it can mean adding more services, or providing services to more people (or both). If you create and sell products, it can come in the form of adding new products, or getting more products to more people (or both).

Self-Love Step

Schedule a quarterly "where are we going session" to figure out where you are in meeting your business goals, what your next steps are, and if any of those goals have changed or been completed. Take note of places where you might need extra help, and congratulate yourself on places where things are running smoothly.

When you allow yourself to be surrounded by a team of awesome people, who are working for your best interests, it also allows you to get away from your business now and then. This is great for a few reasons. First off, it allows you space to think of where you want your business to go. When your head is in the game all the time, it can be hard to think of your next move. Secondly, it frees up your time, so you can spend it on something other than work, which leads me to the next reason building a team for your business is important.

It's Important for the Health of Your Relationships

When you have a team taking some of the stress of your to-do list, it allows you to spend face-to-face time with the ones who love you and are supporting you through your business endeavor.

What does this mean for you? It means you can take time off for family vacation. It means you take days off when you're sick (not just deathly ill). It means you can take a day off for "mental health" (or to celebrate "Mama Needs Chocolate Day"). It means no more missed recitals or plays, or working through your child's baseball game.

Self-Love Step

Schedule at least one day off each week. Scheduling at least two would be even better. Let your team know what you want handled on those days, and just enjoy the peace and the freedom to relax, which leads me to the next reason building a team is important.

It's Important for Your Health

When you work all the time, it can cause fatigue, stress, frustration, etc. All work and no play can make Mama a grumpy bear indeed. It's important to take time for yourself. As important as it is to make time for friends and family, it's equally important to have time just for you.

I know the standard advice is to have a scheduled mani and pedi. That doesn't work for everyone though, so please don't feel like it's your only option. People who work with their hands don't always want manicures, because they won't last. I very rarely get my nails done, simply because I'm usually too antsy to sit there that long. I always mess them up by getting paint or something on them, and I don't like the smell of salons.

That having been said, I really enjoy long hot baths with lavender Epsom salts. I usually take my iPad with me, and listen to music, or catch up on blog feeds, or play games.

Self-Love Step

Schedule a day just for you. Try for at least twice a month. Get your nails done if that's your thing. Get a massage. Go see a movie. Do something that makes you deliriously happy, for no other reason than it makes you deliriously happy.

A team isn't about adding to your work; it's about reducing it. It's not about tying you down; it's about setting you free. And that is precisely why we got into business in the first place!

So whether you've never considered a team, or you've already got your team started, congratulations on your business endeavor! Make sure that you're using your team to its full potential, so that you can reach *your* full potential. Take time for your family and friends, and take time just for you.

About Amanda Sue Howell

Amanda Sue is a visionary, a creator, and a muncher of sour candies. She likes her photography macro, her chocolate dark, and her soda in garish bright green. She's the mother of four amazing children, and she's the wife of a fellow veteran of the *United States Air Force*. Her multiple passions include coaching quirky creatives, correcting grammar, learning new crafts, photography, singing, and of course family. She also hates talking in third person.

Find out more about Amanda Sue Howell on her website: AmandaSueHowell.com

♥

"Loving Yourself First" Note on Simplicity

"That's been one of my mantras—focus & simplicity. Simple can be harder than complex: you have to work hard to get your thinking clean to make it simple. But it's worth it in the end because once you get there, you can move mountains."

-Steve Jobs

You love yourself first when you simplify your life to the degree that you feel focused, purposeful, and generally in control.

Creating simplicity in your life and work can be one of the most challenging endeavors you take on, but it will probably be your most rewarding. The power you gain from it can propel you quickly into a very productive, joyful, and successful life.

Yet editing things out may not be your strong suite. Are you a creative spirit? Do you want to embrace *every* good thing? Do you have the ability (which works overtime) to come up with a variety of wonderful ideas and concepts for your business—ideas that can increase your influence and really help a lot of people in your work?

If you are like many entrepreneurs, simplifying is always a challenge. You are a dynamic, multi-faceted individual with many talents, skills, inner gifts, and interests, and an array of life experiences too. You want to create an exciting life and career, and you certainly don't want to get bored by limiting yourself in any way!

One minute you may want to do one thing, and the next minute you may be on to something else. You want to do a little of this and a little of that; in your work, your entrepreneurial spirit is constantly swirling around within you, enticing you to offer many different things to many kinds of people. In your life, your need for variety has you pulled in way too many directions. You never get the results you *really* want, but still, you keep up the "gotta do it all" pace.

But you know better, don't you? You know that to move forward and create a thriving business or ministry; design exciting and memorable experiences; cultivate lasting and quality relationships; and provide exceptional products and services, you can't be running in a hundred different directions. You must focus!

No matter how much time, money, or resources we have, we just cannot do everything and expect to fully enjoy our life and work.

What you *must* come to know once and for all, is that streamlining does *not* take anything good away from your existence. Quite the opposite is true; simplifying actually opens the door to a life of fullness! When your life is clean and clear, you are more awake, and all of your senses are much more keen, allowing you to connect more richly and deeply to all of your experiences, and to people, too.

The path to simplicity begins with a bit of self-reflection. It starts out by you considering what type of life and work make the most sense to you, *at this time and during this season*, and what in your life, is most meaningful to you. Once you identify that, you can spend your time contributing to and refining those things.

When you clear the clutter in life, you make room for what is most pure and meaningful. It's hard to connect with the "real you" or become aligned with your true passion, purpose, and calling when you are overwhelmed with muck, yuck, and unnecessary activity.

Keep life and business clean! Everything you do in your personal life should be to experience the highest levels of peace, joy, meaning, and interaction with others. Everything you do in your business, ministry, or community should have a specific purpose; a thought-out plan of action; and specified, expected results (so you can measure those results and adjust in case you don't realize them). This keeps you from burning out physically and emotionally with "activity overdo." It also keeps you from wasting time and resources.

Simplicity is a gift, and within it is tremendous power. Simplicity is exciting—never boring. The process to get there takes effort, but it is quite enlightening, and once focused, you gain the freedom to influence your world and make an impact, as you live out your calling and purpose every day.

Lisa Rehurek, the Writer of Chapter 9

I love Lisa! She is all about enjoying life to the fullest. Lisa is a girl who loves people and loves to have fun, and because simplicity is her mantra, she leaves plenty of room in her life for both! She is creative, caring, warm, and stylish, and when you meet her, you are just totally drawn to her!

So many people feel overwhelmed with all they think they have to do. They often feel that life and business are, as Lisa says, "sucking the life out of them." If there is anyone passionate about helping people in this boat, it's Lisa Rehurek. She has the knowledge, skills, and experience, to completely transform lives.

Lisa knows what it takes for a business owner to get their time under control, and she can help you manage your life and business so you can focus on those activities that will move you forward quickly. I call this getting "the biggest bling for your buck"!

If you want to do brilliant work with a calm and peaceful head and heart—that are not pulled in a hundred different directions—then get to know Lisa. She will make certain you are empowered to grow, succeed, and expand your life-work while loving yourself first!

Margo DeGange

♥

Chapter 9
Choose Simplicity:
Five Keys to Living an Uncomplicated Life

By Lisa Rehurek, Business Mentor, Speaker,
International Best-Selling Author

Life is complicated. It seems to get more muddled as we gain access to technologies that are supposed to be designed to make things simpler. We are busier than ever. Relationships are complicated, our family lives are more complex, and our professional lives demand more of us. So how on earth are we supposed to live an uncomplicated life? Complication is thrust upon us without us even realizing it. We feel the pull of the quicksand but don't even notice the rope that is there for the taking. We can't slow down enough to conjure up the energy to un-complicate it.

Or so we think.

Imagine for a moment that you are living life on your own terms—that you are in control, you are ahead of the game, and you get to call the shots. Do you know people like that? They seem to have it all together, and they're never rushed. It's an idealistic life, and it feels so far out of your reach.

What if I told you that you can live that life? That it is a choice, and all you have to do is make the decision to step into it?

For some reason, many of us have been trained to believe that putting ourselves first is a bad thing, that it's selfish. If you spend so much of your time doing things for other people, fulfilling their needs, you end up with little time left to take care of your own needs. Then you get overwhelmed, and in the end your own energy is completely depleted and you feel unfulfilled. Who wins in that scenario? No one! You have nothing left to give to yourself or the people you love most. It's time to take control of your own well-being, to put yourself first so that everyone around you will reap even bigger rewards through your fulfillment.

My passion for sharing this with you comes from a lifetime of trying to live my life on everyone else's terms. It wasn't that anyone in particular was forcing me down a certain path, but I was putting that pressure on myself. I watched people around me, I listened to society, and I allowed outside influences to guide me, instead of listening to my gut. I fought it every step of the way, but it took me a long time to discover that I wasn't fulfilled. I knew I didn't always want to do things the way everyone else does them. And it dawned on me one day, that that's okay. I realized that this is *my* life, and no one else's. Who gets to define what fulfillment is in *my* life? I do! No one else is going to look out for me the way *I'll* look out for me. And so it began, my quest for living my life on my own terms.

What I discovered is that my life is so much simpler now that I know what I want. And I find that I have more to give those around me, because I am happier and more fulfilled. When we don't know where we're going, or why we're headed there, we can't weed out the people, places, and things that are not serving us. So we end up taking on so much more than we need to. That's when our lives become complicated. If you can get grounded in your own vision, in your own truth, you will start to feel some relief.

The five strategies that follow will allow that kind of contentment and proactivity into your life, if you choose to embrace them. As you move through these five strategies, you can choose to apply them to your personal and/or professional life. Ultimately, you will want to apply them to both to reap maximum reward.

Key #1 Seek Awareness

What is your mind telling you? What stories do you tell yourself? Which of those stories are serving you, and which are sabotaging you? What do you need to let go of and adjust?

Being aware and in tune is the first step to making lasting changes in your life. If you don't like where you are, then seek awareness of the changes that need to take place. Full awareness of exactly where you are is imperative in order to move to the next stage, to truly make a lasting change.

Self-Love Step

The best way to gain awareness is to journal. Journal your thoughts, your beliefs, and your emotions. When you put pen to paper, it's much easier to see how these thoughts and beliefs are helping or hindering you. You start to see patterns, and see vividly the stories that you tell yourself. The more open you are to discovering which stories might not be serving you, the quicker you can face them head on, and move past them.

This strategy is simply about becoming aware of your thought patterns, of those stories that are embedded in your brain, and that steer your decisions and actions. Gaining this deep understanding of what your thoughts are, and what beliefs and emotions are guiding you, will allow you to make the necessary shifts. You cannot change the things of which you are unaware.

Key #2   Move Towards Acceptance

Once you are aware, you can move toward acceptance. You must be willing to accept those things in your life that you need to change: the mental stories that you've been holding on to, and any excuses or victim mentality that you have been unaware of until now. We move from awareness to acceptance because it's one thing to be aware of where your mind is directing you, and it's another to accept that some of those emotions and beliefs are doing you more harm than good. Then and only then can you make a lasting change.

Self-Love Step

Learn to accept! This is probably the hardest step for people; accepting that things can be different, and accepting that they should be different.

Let's face it; most people don't like change, even if it means wallowing in burden and discomfort. The fear of the unknown is far more treacherous than the muck we're living in. We are martyrs. We believe that no one is as "unique" as we are, and we think our situations are "different." Are we making excuses or is that reality? We live in denial most of the time, and we don't want to accept that maybe the thoughts in our minds are derailing us.

It's true for most people, but if you're reading this, you're not most people. You're ready to step out and make a change. You're ready to breathe again, to fill your bucket and feel fulfilled, and to live that life you know you deserve.

Togetheer, awareness and acceptance become the foundation for everything else you do. Without working through them, you will almost always struggle with forward progress toward your goals. You need your actions to be sustainable so you can get to the end result, which is Success.

Allow me to share with you my magic success formula:

$$(\textbf{Awareness} + \textbf{Acceptance}) + \textbf{Action} = \textbf{Success}^{\text{TM}}$$

How do you define success? It may mean losing 20 pounds. It could be making more money. Or it just might be as simple as laughing every day. You can define success however you like, whether it's for your personal or professional life. The formula for getting there doesn't change based on that definition.

Key #3   Find Clarity

Once you eliminate the mental blocks that are holding you back, it's time to get clear on your purpose and passion and let go of the clutter and noise that is depleting you.

Finding clarity is about knowing what you want and need, and defining your purpose and your passion. It can feel like a selfish endeavor at times. It is about finding what is right for *you* and only you.

Self-Love Step

What makes *you* happy, or in the words of a good friend, what "melts your butter?" What fire in your belly will get you springing out of bed in the morning with a huge smile on your face? Determine this.

It is so beautiful when you are aware of what your mind is controlling, and you can accept that you need to make some changes. All of a sudden you can see clearly for the first time in a long time. You have eliminated the stubbornness that comes with holding on and not accepting change. You can finally see what is truly beautiful to you, what makes your heart pound so hard you feel like it's going to leap over the highest mountain. That is the feeling we need to strive for every day. And trust me, it does exist!

You have a passion deep inside of you, and it is time to find it again. Get clear on what that passion is. And remember, this is all about you, baby! You must take care of yourself before you can give the best you've got to anyone else. So get clear on what is important to *you*.

Key #4   Eliminate Complexity

You've become aware, you've accepted the fact that some of your internal messages need to change, and now you know what you want. The next step is to clear out the complications in your daily life that toss you into overwhelm.

Do you feel like you make things more complicated than they need to be? I fall into that trap sometimes myself. If something feels too complicated and cluttered, it probably *is* too complicated. Obvious? Not always!

Self-Love Step

Here are some simple questions you can ask yourself when you find you're overwhelmed with complexity in your daily activities:

♥   Why am I doing this? There may be reasons you did things a certain way at some point, but those reasons may no longer serve you. Make sure there is a valuable reason for doing the things you are doing.

♥ Is there an easier way to do it? There almost always is. Get help, or get another set of eyes on it. Sometimes you can't see clearly when you're too close to it.

♥ How does this serve me? Is this activity tied to your passion and purpose? The majority of the time, it should be. If it isn't, then why are you doing it?

♥ Who is this benefiting? If the activity isn't truly benefiting you or those closest to you, why are you doing it?

♥ Does this make my heart sing? If the answer to this question is "No" more than it is "Yes," you need to re-evaluate.

Make this a consistent practice and you will start to eliminate the unnecessary complexities in your everyday life.

Key #5 Live in Simplicity

All of the previous steps are setting you up to live a life of simplicity. We've talked about building a foundation for ridding yourself of the mindset that no longer serves you. You've moved into acceptance so you can make the necessary changes. You are now clear on your purpose and passion, and you have some tools to help you avoid the complexities that pop up in your daily activities. The previous strategies are all setting you up to be able to embrace simplicity.

Self-Love Step

My four basic rules to achieve simplicity include:

Rule #1   Be present, and your relationships will be stronger and more fulfilling.

Rule #2   Listen, and your interactions will be more rewarding.

Rule #3   Be grateful, and your days will be filled with more happiness.

Rule #4   Slow down, and you will feel more joy, love, and happiness.

It's your choice. Only you can make that decision. Choose simplicity and live life on your terms.

Now that you've read through these five strategies, you know what the end game is. Remember, the intention is to gain simplicity and remove as much complication as possible. So start small, take it one step at a time, beginning with awareness. Once you feel you've mastered that, move on to the next strategy.

This won't happen overnight, and it should become an ongoing part of your daily life. I personally review these strategies regularly to regroup, and to make sure I'm grounded in simplicity. I hope you do the same.

About Lisa Rehurek

Lisa Rehurek is a speaker, author, and business mentor, and she teaches entrepreneurs how to develop a strategy, get stuff done, and make more money. Lisa has a super diverse background, spending 20 years in various industries in the corporate world. She has founded/co-founded five businesses, including her current six-figure business, *MissSimplicity*. Lisa has a passion for helping women entrepreneurs live their lives *their* way.

Find out more about Lisa Rehurek on her website: Miss-Simplicity.com

♥

"Loving Yourself First" Note on Supportive Spaces

*"Interiors should not be about trends;
they should be about people and how they live."*

-James Huniford

Have you ever gone to a coffee shop or café to have some quiet time and get a bit of work done? Most of us have. Have you ever left a coffee shop or café earlier than expected because the environment was not comfortable to you for some reason, and so it did not support you in your task at hand? I think a lot of people have. Often, if your environment doesn't look attractive, isn't set at the right temperature, doesn't have an acceptable or pleasant smell, or isn't set up to function well, it becomes a place of distraction.

Our interior spaces are very much a part of who we are, and contribute greatly to how we show up in the world. When we live and work in spaces that impact us in positive ways, it empowers us. Our spaces become a springboard for personal and professional success.

Part of lifestyle design is interior design, and not simply for the sake of beauty and aesthetics. Good design looks great, yes, but it also supports the soul and the psyche. Designing each of your spaces with a clear and definite purpose can add richness and substance to the experience of your life.

If you travel frequently for work, for example, you can design a bedroom for more than just sleep. It can become a retreat-like refuge that engulfs you and helps you fully decompress and refresh when you are at home. If you are a home-based entrepreneur, your home office space can be strategically and brilliantly designed to help you reach very specific business goals. Your office can become a place that fosters measurable productivity, or it can be an environment where the limits to your creative process are taken away!

Great design can increase your joy and productivity and improve how you interact and connect with others. Overall, it can greatly improve how you feel and how you live. That is powerful! Meaningful and intentional design leads to interiors that thoroughly support the way you choose to live and work every day.

This type of smart design does not have to be expensive. It starts with knowing what you want from your spaces, and designing from that vantage point. Then (and not until then, actually) the aesthetics come into play. The personally meaningful use of specific design elements such as color, pattern, texture, sound, and fragrance for example, coupled with the skillful use of design principles such as placement, balance, unity and contrast, to name just a few, can totally transform a room. Then, as budget allows, items like furnishings, fabrics, surfaces, and lighting fixtures can be chosen based on personal taste and preferences to further enhance a space.

As business owners and individuals who do important life-work, we owe ourselves interiors that help to fill our senses, trigger our genius, advance our missions, and add to our overall happiness. Begin today to design spaces that support you in how you envision yourself living and working each and every day. You have the power, through your interior design, to create the life that means so much to you!

Sherry Burton Ways, the Writer of Chapter 10

Sherry Burton Ways is woman with vision, and in everything she does, she looks beyond to see how it all fits together. For an Interior Designer, this is an enviable trait. No wonder her clients love her so much. They trust that as she creates their living and work spaces, she will always factor in each and every aspect of the big picture to form a cohesive whole. Sherry designs for true balance and harmony.

Sherry does not stop at only designing spaces full of meaning. Her friendships and business relationships are full of meaning too! She is purposeful in all that she does, and people matter a great deal to her. Her life and her work reflect that. She is a joy to work with because she is not only skilled, but caring, and warm.

With no shortage of credentials, talents, and expertise, Sherry is a very distinguished professional. I know she values education and life-long learning, and she never quits conquering new disciplines that will help her clients create amazing spaces that foster very full lives.

The words on the following pages come from Sherry's heart and from her skill and wisdom too. Let them speak to you so you can make the changes in your home, office, and life that you may have been putting off. Through her instruction, expect to grow and to be elevated to new and invigorating heights. She can help you configure a life and home on purpose, as your confidence increases and your self-esteem begins to soar!

Margo DeGange

♥

Chapter 10
Supportive Spaces
By Sherry Burton Ways,
Certified Feng Shui and Design Expert

You are on the run from morning until night. To maintain your sanity, you have to be able to wind down and relax once you return home after an action-packed day. But in today's world of e-mails, Twitter, LinkedIn, and Facebook, it's tough to relax and let the external world melt away.

There was a time in my life when I would work all day in a non-supportive environment, and then come home to a space where I felt uninspired. To overcome that, I knew I had to do something to support my well-being, self-care, and love for myself, so that I would be able to face the next day. To do this, I searched my soul, read decorating books, magazines, and anything else I could get my hands on, to inspire me to create a home environment that relieved my stress, and supported my life in my work-place outside of the home.

I went back to my roots. Inspired by ethnic design and colors, I created a haven for myself that did more than provide an aesthetically pleasing environment. I decorated my home using colors and themes from the African continent. Through this self-discovery and journey, I was called to create a celebratory experience to reinforce my culture and my self. As a result, my home became my own private supportive space that reinforced my being, and captivated self-love at the same time.

Your Personal Self-Love Through Supportive Space

Part of your personal self-care and self-love is to live and work in a supportive space. What is a supportive space? My definition is any space where your essential sense of self can be expressed. It is a private place where you are inspired by colors, textures, sights, sounds, and aromas.

Your home environment should be the place where you place the external world in check and leave your stressors outside your front door. Therefore, the need for a supportive interior environment should be paramount in your journey of peace, balance, and tranquility in your life.

Our Homes do Several Things for Us:

- ♥ They provide us a haven for peace and tranquility.

- ♥ They provide support for our outer social harmony and inner personal harmony.

- ♥ They reflect our attitudes and beliefs.

- ♥ They are the environments where we have total control.

When we are fixated on decorating our spaces based on principles, or on creating an "energetically perfect space," we shortchange ourselves. Why? Because then we let society, HGTV, and high-end design magazines, etc., tell us what we should or should not do in our spaces.

Supportive space is important for self-care. Here are some key insights I have come to discover:

1. As humans, we long for our own personal space to relax, regroup, and indulge.

2. It is good Feng Shui to create a space for peace of mind and meditation in our homes.

3. Many people—women in particular—do not create a supportive space of their own in their homes.

Now is the time to create a space that is about *you* and *you only*. It is not your neighbor's space, and it is not about trying to keep up with the latest design trends. It is about who you are and your place in the universe!

Think about what your decor' is or is not. What is it that you want it to be? *Now get out of your own way,* and in your space, create the feeling you were born to align with! I promise, you will create the space you love, with ease and beauty!

Does your home feel calm and restful? Or is it cluttered and chaotic, just like everything you're trying to escape? If it is the latter, it may be time to Feng Shui your home.

Excuses for Not Creating a Supportive Space

We all have reasons why we can or cannot create a supportive space for ourselves. However, for your personal well-being and as part of loving yourself, a supportive space is essential. Here are some common excuses for not creating one:

♥   We are already lacking space for our family. I cannot take a space to support myself.

♥ It is impractical to create another space in our home. I simply cannot afford it.

♥ It is a luxury to create a supportive space in my home for myself. It is so selfish to think of doing that.

♥ I really have no idea where to begin.

Understanding Feng Shui and Supportive Spaces

An ancient Chinese art of placement, Feng Shui—which translates literally to "wind" and "water"—is about balancing the energy, or chi, of a living space and its inhabitants, to increase well-being in all aspects, such as health, prosperity, relationships, career, etc. The goal of Feng Shui is to create constant, mutual interaction between your personal energy and your environment. Each continually affects and shapes the other.

According to Feng Shui principles, elements such as colors, sounds, and symbols—along with how you arrange furniture and other items—are instrumental in creating a pleasing indoor environment.

There are five cardinal rules of Feng Shui that anyone can use without becoming a Feng Shui Master:

1. Clear the clutter.

2. Create Zen (clear) surfaces.

3. Rid yourself of things you do not love.

4. Remove or replace broken items.

5. Create a sacred, reverent quiet space.

When you inhabit a living space that has healthy *chi,* or good energy, your own life force is enhanced and preserved.

The Elements of Creating Supportive Spaces

Taken from the history and principles of Feng Shui, I narrowed down three elements to creating a supportive space:

1. De-clutter your space.

2. Choose therapeutic colors.

3. Integrate natural elements into the space.

De-clutter Your Space

Clutter is a primary obstacle to positive chi. Whether it's an ever-mounting pile of mail or a shelf full of disorganized, dust-caked CDs, clutter constantly reminds you that you've left something—or several things—unfinished. The result for many is anxiety and restlessness.

To "Zen" your space, remove any items you no longer use, and don't let your kids drop their backpacks in the doorway.

Repair any damaged items in your space. If you have broken windows, pipes, vases, or anything, chi circulates and then sits there. This has the same negative effect as clutter because it does nothing to uplift the space or its occupants—it's negative Feng Shui.

Choose Therapeutic Colors

Research shows different colors evoke different feelings. Colors vibrate at various electromagnetic frequencies, which can make people feel either energetically harmonious or dissonant.

According to color psychology, bright reds and yellows can cause agitation and anxiety, while blues, purples, and greens are calming. Therefore, paint walls and decorate with cool shades, to create a stress-reducing interior.

For example, the color green stimulates feelings of harmony, peace, hope, growth, and healing. Blue is excellent for bedrooms and rooms where meditation is practiced, and purples are equally soothing because they're tied to awareness and intuition.

The colors and images in your decor' reflect aspects of yourself that can build you up or tear you down. Color can nurture your soul as food nourishes your body. Determine which colors are your favorites and which ones feed you.

The best way to learn about the effect of colors is to look at those we choose in our home environments. These give many clues to our personalities and inner feelings. Carefully chosen colors can build our self-image so that we are better able to cope with the stresses of modern life, and improve our relationships with others.

Color preferences coincide with major changes in our lives, and a change in attitude or physical state is often accompanied by a change in our color preferences. Think about one of your favorite rooms in your house. Which colors are mostly in that room? Do these colors uplift you or make you feel depressed? Find colors that make you feel good.

Integrate Natural Elements Into the Space

To achieve balance within a room, incorporate each of the five Chinese elements: earth, fire, metal, water, and wood. These can be represented through textures, shapes, and colors. For instance, to personify water without literally bringing it in, incorporate dark, shiny, reflective surfaces and fabrics with wave-like patterns.

Symbols of nature provoke inner harmony and allow you to achieve your desired mood. To cultivate calm, complement a predominantly blue living room with sand-colored throw pillows or an end table fashioned from unfinished wood. Plants, too, bring life and positive chi to a room—just avoid ones with pointed leaves, which can encourage sharp negative energy in a space.

In addition, here are a few more ways you can decorate your supportive space using materials that are earth friendly:

- ♥ Use low or no-VOC paint products, and paint your own walls.

- ♥ Use recycled fabric to reupholster existing furniture.

- ♥ Use the items that you already own to decorate your space.

- ♥ Shop for additional items at yard sales, consignment shops, and flea markets for lighting, furniture, tables, and other items.

Handmade items help to bring in sentimental feelings, and evoke memories of the past. Items that have been crafted, crocheted, and quilted bring colors, patterns, and textures to our interiors that remind us of the past, and help us reflect and refocus during times of socioeconomic crises.

Consider your supportive space as a place to demonstrate the need for conserving the environment.

Your Supportive Space

To create an interior environment that supports your personal and professional goals, it is best to create a home environment that fully supports the way you want to be, and the way you want to live in the world. So as you prepare mentally and spiritually for this exciting *shift*, your home or office interior must be in alignment for the abundance prepared for you. To prepare your interior for the *shift*, here are six strategies:

1. Discover your personal (and even professional) needs and goals.

2. Create an action plan for setting up your interior environment so that these needs and goals will be supported and fully realized.

3. Consider spaces that integrate personal hobbies, work, and creativity into your home.

4. Incorporate design elements that can have an emotional and psychological effect on your well-being and productivity, both within the home and outside of it.

5. Know what your personal development colors are and how to integrate them into your interior. There is

nothing like having the right customized colors in your environment to help you thrive at your highest level.

6. Learn about the Feng Shui five elements for balancing a space.

There are no rules for the creation of a supportive space. You can create or design one in any way that you want, for any purpose, and in any size or location. You don't need a lot of room to create a supportive space.

This is your time to think about making a shift in your mindset about your interior. In order to prepare, you will need more spiritual and energetic tools. Listen to your intuition and be in touch with your spiritual self. It is about moving to action instead of waiting for permission to move forward.

Self-Love Steps

1. Identify a space in your home where you spend the most time. Describe it:

> What is it that you like about it?

> What makes it sacred?

> Did you decorate it, or did it evolve organically?

2. If you don't have a space, think about your ideal supportive space and what you would do in it.

Through understanding our personal color choices, Feng Shui, and preferences in our interiors, we find that we can influence our self-expression. In addition, by incorporating personal accents into our spaces (taken from historical traditions that we feel most in common with), we can create something that is truly our own. Creating supportive spaces helps to improve our health, enhances our relationships, and promotes peace of mind.

About Sherry Burton Ways

As the principal and CEO of the Washington, D.C. based *Kreative Ways & Solutions, LLC,* Sherry Burton Ways is a Certified Feng Shui Re-designer, Certified Interior Environment Coach, Interior Color Therapist, and Holistic Interior Designer who designs soul-satisfying spaces. She assists her clients to understand what is blocking them in their lives, by looking at the spaces they occupy and the colors with which they surround themselves.

Find out more about Sherry Burton Ways on her website: SherryBurtonWays.com

♥

"Loving Yourself First" Note on Our Homes

"Design is coming to grips with one's real lifestyle, one's real place in the world. Rooms should not be put together for show but to nourish one's wellbeing."

-Albert Hadley

I have been stating for years that our home is a very real extension and expression of who we are at our core. How we chose to live within our homes; how we function at home day to day; how we communicate and connect within the walls; and how we set up and display the elements and items in our rooms and spaces, says so much about us.

How you live in your home reflects how you see life, and also how you see, and feel about, yourself. I could peek through a window of your home, and in a sense, I would be taking a look into your soul.

If your kitchen pantry and fridge hold an array of unhealthy foods, I would probably not be far off in thinking that you are putting yourself last and your health on hold. If your bedroom is a mess, with uncomfortable bedding and a TV that is turned on every night, I might be safe to suggest you do not get the rest you need on a regular basis. If there are mini-messes and piles everywhere in your rooms, I could likely conclude that you are either overwhelmed in your work, or you're too busy to manage what's currently in your life. If your furnishings are placed haphazardly or arranged awkwardly, and the placement makes you uneasy, I would undoubtedly be correct in assuming you feel disconnected to life in some way. If you can never find what you need in your home when you need it, you might agree that you feel somewhat out of control in some area of your life.

You can't fix all of your problems in a day. You can't deal with all of life's hiccups at one time, and make them suddenly disappear, but you can work the equation backwards and still come to an empowering solution: you can spearhead a deliberately designed life by the way you set up your home. You can create systems and ideal interior environments that make you feel fabulous, and therefore help you to function better all around. So instead of fixing all the issues in your life, why not fix your home environment? Why not design from the perspective of who you want to be, how you want to live, how you want to feel, how you want to relate, and what kind of world view you want to embrace?

Set the home up for your optimum health and wellness, for organization and order, for creating memories and meaningful relationships, and for experiencing love and beauty, and you will be changed through it! When your home environment is initially created and regularly maintained to support abundance, love, wholeness, and success, you will cease to struggle to behave like the person you know you were meant to be. Instead, you will *become* that person, the one you truly are!

Nancy Meadows, the Writer of Chapter 11

Nancy Meadows is one of my all time favorite people! She is rather chic and sophisticated, and seems to have a real grasp on how to live a life filled with purpose and beauty. She is deliberate. She is intentional. She is brilliant, actually, because she "sees" very clearly, and hones in on the most important and precious things about life and work. She approaches them both the same way she approaches interior design—*mindfully!*

One thing I know for certain about Nancy: she does not lose perspective. She has such command of what feels best for her, and she knows where the boundary line is between enough and too much. She seems to be always led by a sense of peace.

Any client who works with Nancy will be transformed. Her entire philosophy of design is holistic. It requires you to look at who you are, how you feel, and how you want to live, so that you can be all that you know is possible, and experience life to the fullest. Nancy understands the power of the home to uplift, support, heal, and inspire. She is a *fantastic* interior designer!

On a personal level, Nancy is a fabulous person to talk with—so down to earth, but in the most elegant sort of way! She is incredibly kind and caring, and light-hearted, too (with a great laugh). I feel so very blessed to have her in my life!

Margo DeGange

♥
Chapter 11
Home as a Touchstone: Balancing Your Professional and Private Worlds

By Nancy Meadows, Lifestyle Interior Designer and
Certified Interior Environment Coach

You may wonder how living your best life at home can have a major, even profound affect on how well you navigate your professional life. Who we are at home is not necessarily who we are out in the world, and yet they are intrinsically linked. We play different roles depending on the situation in which we find ourselves, but just like our bodies are made up of different parts, they all work together to function as a whole, each in harmony with the other. So it is with our work and home lives.

According to organizational psychologist David Wellington, Ph.D., "Work is inherently stressful. There are psychological demands of interacting with other people, meeting deadlines and performing. We need breaks . . . to recover, reboot."

This is the role our home can play. It's the one place where we are truly free to be ourselves, where we foster dreams, and understand who we are now, and where we want to go as we grow into who we will become. In essence, home is our touchstone.

As a lifestyle interior designer, my clients are often faced with the challenge of this balancing act. How do we merge the various parts of ourselves into a harmonious whole?

Amy's Story

Amy (not her real name) is a client with whom I worked several years ago. She was the head of an advertising agency. Amy's work world was frantic and fast-paced. A large part of her job was dealing with ego-driven creative people, not to mention the clients who demanded results for their advertising dollars. Amy came to me because she wasn't able to relax at home, and she desperately wanted and needed to change.

During a walk-through of her home, I noticed job-related papers strewn across her dining room table. The colors she chose for her walls were bright; the furniture coverings were busy prints; and accessories seemed to be everywhere. In many ways, it echoed the atmosphere of her work environment. She had brought it home with her, and it was no wonder she felt anxious. As a result, she wasn't able to connect with her soul-self.

Sally's Story

Another client, Sally, experienced the opposite situation. She was a research assistant and worked alone in a small office that afforded little interaction with colleagues. Although she loved her work, it was solitary, and her home reflected the same quiet state. It had a Zen-like quality that, for Sally, wasn't working. She needed stimulation—brighter colors and places for easy socializing with friends.

Ironically, both Amy and Sally would have probably received psychological relief by exchanging their home environments. Amy would have benefited from the tranquility of Sally's place, whereas Sally needed the vibrancy, the aliveness, even some of the messiness, of Amy's home.

Home as Haven

Our home offers so much more than mere shelter. It can be that loving friend who welcomes you at the end of the day. James Yandell, M.D., Ph.D., former President of the Jung Institute of San Francisco, noted the following: "A right home can protect, heal, and restore us; express who we are now; and over time help us become who we are meant to be." When we think of our homes in those terms, it's not difficult to know if we're in harmony with ourselves. Indeed, we carry that sense of wholeness and balance with us into the world where we live our professional lives.

Our home environment is one we create and control. We don't always have that option in our professional lives, where making the best of a situation is sometimes all we can do. At home we can almost be like children again, living in our imagination and dreaming of all the possibilities, giving our subconscious self free rein to burst forth.

What the World Expects

Our western cultural beliefs typically overrate concepts associated with achievement, and they underrate the quality of experience and connection with personal values. Consequently, that's all the more reason that our home becomes the place where we can psychologically rebalance ourselves, and where we can attain perfect synchrony. When we think of traditional interior design, what comes to mind is how a space looks and whether it performs well. Both style and function are important, but what about the interior of our "self"—the place where we really live? When we are able to connect the two, there is a sense of self-empowerment that we share with the world.

Branding Our Home

Most business people understand the term *branding*. We know that it creates a clear and memorable impression about who we are and what our business is about. It communicates our values and abilities, whether we are a small business owner, a solo-preneur, or a corporate executive. We can mindfully do the same in our home. We can define who we are, what is truly important to us, and what makes us unique. From there we can identify exactly how our home needs to serve us in order to thrive inside and outside of our home.

Allison's Story:
Successful Professionally, But Not Personally

Another client, Allison, also came to me because she was having trouble balancing her career world with her personal one. She had spent years working her way up the corporate ladder with great success. Even so, she felt incomplete, as if something was missing and limiting her sense of wholeness. She loved her place but wasn't connecting with it. It was an address more than it was "home." It protected her physically but didn't fulfill her emotionally. She had reached a transition point that required change to enhance her life.

As I do with all of my clients, Allison and I initially worked through a series of questions, assessments, and exercises that had nothing to do with traditional interior design. On the contrary, it had everything to do with who she really was at her core. We discovered what she psychologically needed, so she could live in total harmony with her professional and personal environment in the deepest possible way. Some of what we probed is described below.

Six Mindful Ways to Create a Home Environment That Empowers Your Professional Life

It doesn't matter whether you live in a studio apartment or a 10,000-square-foot mansion. The objective is to mindfully create spaces that envelop your heart, soul, and mind to live your best self every day in every way. Here are some simple but effective steps to follow.

Self-Love Steps

1. While walking through your home, visually step outside of the box and look at things as though it was the first time you've seen them. This is important because when we see something every day, we no longer "see" it. It becomes an invisible part of the landscape. It may seem extreme, but sometimes it helps to remove furniture and accessories from a room to see it with fresh eyes.

2. Take photos of each room. This is another way to view your space in a more detached manner. Look at your photos and write down your first impressions. Don't concentrate too much, because your mind will start filtering, and won't reflect your true feelings. We do this all the time. Our mind is our "head place" which undoubtedly serves an important function. But the "heart place" is where our dreams live. Our first thoughts on anything can also be called intuition, or gut feelings. This is our built-in GPS. It tells us what we really think on a subconscious level. With our heart space, we say "What if?" Our head space tells us "You can't because . . ."

3. When you've written your first impressions, think of what you might change or add. Let yourself go, and allow your creativity to flow.

4. Make a spreadsheet with each room listed. Underneath each room, write down the changes you'd like to make. It may be one or many things.

5. Think in terms of how the room functions and (more importantly) how it feels to you. How well does it serve you? What are your most important needs? For example, if you have a formal dining room that you only use at Thanksgiving and Christmas, how about turning that space into one you can use all the time? If reading is your passion, and you love books, why not line the walls with book shelves and use the dining table as a library table? Remember, the whole idea in designing your home is that you live your rooms—not the other way around.

6. At this point, you've visited all of your rooms, and you now have a wish list of the changes you'd like to make. Next, list them in order of preference. What is the most important thing to change right now? Go at your own pace, but prepare action steps, and set a date to start and finish your projects.

If Your Workplace Is Your Home

Special attention must be devoted to working at home, which many of us do. With today's technology, this has become more and more common. While working at home has many advantages, it also carries some pitfalls that must mindfully be avoided. The crucial objective is to create separation of our home and work spaces. Ideally your office is a separate room that can be completely closed off with a door and used for nothing except work. If that's not possible, a screen or even curtains will work. Psychologically, there has to be some kind of barrier that you see, so when you close that door, screen, or curtain, you know that you've left the office and are now back in your sanctuary called home.

Be sure to set a definite time schedule for work, and avoid the temptation to violate it during your free time. The temporal boundaries will serve to complement the physical ones that you've established.

It's also important during the day to give yourself breaks. Take a walk; go to a coffee house; eat lunch out. You need to engage with other people. You'll not only stay refreshed, but you'll be more inspired and productive when you get back to work.

A Final Word

If you follow the above recommendations, I promise you'll look at your home in a different, more positive way. You will change your perspective, feel more confident and clear, and this clarity will carry over into your professional life as well.

Even though we wear different "hats," depending on what role we are playing at the time, there must be a congruency that allows us to feel whole. And this, of course, starts with how we live in our homes—the one place where we have the control and freedom to express ourselves in our most real way. The whole idea is to create a space that allows us to live our most fulfilled selves.

Clare Cooper Marcus aptly stated the following in her book, *House as a Mirror of Self*: "Throughout our lives, we strive for a state of wholly being ourselves. Everything that happens in our life; people, places, experiences, are our teachers. Our places, our homes, are reflections of that process and have a powerful effect on our journey to wholeness."

Your home is the pivot point between your inner and outer worlds. In expanding your horizons, you should strive to gain strength, acceptance, and stability in the inner one. This will make you ready to step out into the outer world of adventure and risk-taking, and survive all of the many peaks and valleys of life.

Home: Where we begin and end.

About Nancy Meadows

Nancy Meadows is a Lifestyle Interior Designer whose focus is working with heartfelt women and how they live in their homes. Practicing *"Mindful Interior Design,"* a method that she developed, empowers women to create transformational living spaces, that give them that instant, instinctive, gut-level reaction that their home feels "just right." Nancy is also a co-author of the international best-selling book, *Success in (High) Heels.*

Find out more about Nancy Meadows on her website: NancyMeadowsDesigns.com

♥

"Loving Yourself First" Note on Setbacks

*"Every new beginning comes from
some other beginning's end."*

-Seneca

Life is full of setbacks. Even when most circumstances in life go relatively smoothly, challenges and obstacles show up. Some are small and easily manageable, while others are colossal, and shake us up so rigorously that we need help from others to get up and get through them.

Although we never see it while we are going through a hard place, trials teach us so much about ourselves, others, and the real purpose of life in general. Often, it's the times of intensity that help us understand more deeply who we are and what we are here to do. It is often life's challenges that trigger us to make important changes and adjustments.

If we allow them to, trials can work greatly for our good and for our increased joy long term, no matter how hard the trial is while we are going though it. Trials test our faith and give us opportunity to show forth the strength that is really in us. Trials help us to see how God shows up for us, too. Trials also teach us patience, and if we let that patience work perfectly in our lives, we will come out on the other side fully complete, lacking nothing, and with tremendous confidence, knowing nothing can ever take us down!

Knowing this, choose to see the joy in your challenges, especially in the small and incidental mishaps that show up daily, which will help prepare you—if you let them—for the great things you are destined to do, and for the strong and confident leader you are becoming day by day.

Laura DeTomaso Smith, the Writer of Chapter 12

The people we love to be around are the ones who use what they've been though to uplift and encourage others. Laura DeTomaso Smith is one of those amazing people. She has chosen a path of optimism and love, and you can see it shine forth in her life and work. Recently I hopped over to her Facebook wall for a visit, and of course I immediately found something positive to help me in my day. It was a video of a 109 year old Holocaust survivor, sharing her secret to a long and happy life. The caption Laura wrote read, "She is amazing. If you watch this you'll feel better in 60 seconds. Love it!"

Laura finds a way to learn, leap forward, and love, no matter the circumstances, and because of that her work is real, full of substance, and deeply meaningful. Not one of us has lived a life without trials, but not all of us have learned to use those trials for inspiration and growth. Laura has!

There's no need to let life's road bumps drain you of your drive and motion, especially not when Laura is in your view! You will find her to be powerfully practical and wonderfully charming, as she helps you to see how all that you face, and all that you have been through in your life, can be the very fuel to deliver you to your destiny!

Margo DeGange

♥
Chapter 12
Getting Your Groovy Back:
May the Force be with You
By Laura DeTomaso Smith,
Chief Groovy Chick at The Breakup Lounge

Act 1- And I Found Myself Single. Again!

Have you been there too? You think you have your future figured out but . . . life happens. Things change and before you know it, you're picking up the pieces and starting over.

For me, this was not my first time at the rodeo. Nope. By the time most people were getting their first divorce, I was a seasoned pro.

Before we go there, let me give you a bit of background. I live in Minnesota. It's the "Land of 10,000 Lakes" and some pretty well-established and preconceived notions. One of these is that it's totally okay to get divorced once but you'd better make that second marriage work. This is one of the reasons I languished in my second marriage for so long. I was not joining "it." "It" was the shameful . . . the embarrassing . . . the *Twice Divorced Club*.

I really struggled with that being part of my new identity. What would people say? What would people think? One part of my personality that didn't help the situation was that I was a bona fide people pleaser. I needed others to feel good about me so I could feel good about myself. Sound familiar?

When you're a people pleaser, the opinions of others become magnified and more important than what you think of yourself. On top of that, do we ever examine said opinions before we accept them? No, ma'am. They have direct VIP access straight to our hearts. It doesn't matter if they're good, bad, or otherwise. There's absolutely no filter to decipher truth.

Despite the looming rejection of others, I initiated divorce proceedings in 2005. Suffice it to say that infidelity just isn't my thing!

After the initial "What the hell just happened to my life?" reaction, I settled into a new and very different normal. For the first time ever, I got to know me, and guess what? I kind of liked her. She was actually a pretty cool chick.

I realized that I was a whole helluva lot stronger than I ever gave myself credit for. I created a life that I loved. In 2009, I became the "Elizabeth Taylor" of Minnesota, when I married for the third time.

Act 2- I Decided to Start a Business

What kind of business did I begin? Not a vegetable stand where no mention of my history was required. Not a daycare where I could coddle little ones all day. No. I wanted to help women with broken hearts get their groovy back. So I decided to start *The Breakup Lounge*. What a great idea, right? Give women who are in my former shoes a shortcut to happiness! Brilliant, huh? Not . . . so . . . fast!

I soon realized that in order to really be authentic and gain trust I would have to do the one thing that completely terrified me, yep—admit to the world that I had been married three times and divorced *twice*.

Basically, it felt like I was broadcasting, "Hey, everybody! Look at me! I'm a huge failure!" I had gone to incredible lengths to protect my "privacy" around this taboo subject and now, I was going to have to surrender to it and own it, and own it with . . . pride? Was that possible?

I knew that, inevitably, I'd have to get out in front of actual living, breathing human beings and lay it all out there, waiting to be judged, hoping to swing in and "people please" before the pain of their judgment swooped in and clobbered my fragile self-esteem.

I kept asking myself, "How will I ever be strong enough to endure the sense of rejection and disapproval? How will I survive?"

What could I possibly do to be "me"—the twice-divorced, thrice-married *me*—without allowing myself to be crippled by shame? How would I keep from absorbing all of the perceived negativity about my past?

If you're an entrepreneur, depending on what you do, I'm sure you can relate. There's a certain raw honesty about ourselves that's required to really succeed.

Also, entrepreneurship has a way of bringing all your "issues" to light. Some you've known about for years. Others surface in surprising ways. Being an entrepreneur really is a course in self-discovery.

Act 3- I had a Crazy Idea that Worked

I knew that I had to figure out a way to shield myself when needed. One day, I was watching *Land Of The Lost* with my family. If you've never heard of it, it's a movie with Will Ferrell that's a remake of an old 70s kids' show. There's a family that accidentally travels back in time to the prehistoric era. They find themselves fighting off dinosaurs, Sleestaks (alien-like creatures), and a host of other threatening predators. If they rubbed two particular crystals together, they created a temporary "force field" of protection.

Then it hit me, "Why don't I create my *own* personal force field? How helpful would that be?" What if I could call up my force field at will? What if I could use it with anyone in any situation? I could protect myself and *be* myself at the same time. It would allow me to feel safe in my vulnerability as I went out into the world and showed everyone in it the real me. It was worth a try. Let me share with you what that looked like.

Self-Love Steps

1. Imagine that you have a beautiful glowing force field around your entire body. You can make it whatever color you like. Allow yourself to feel protected by it. It's truly your shield from the outside world. Also, you can choose to slide it open and admit genuinely helpful things at will. I picture mine as having sliding doors in front of my chest. It feels powerful.

2. Live your life. Undoubtedly, as you go through your day, you will encounter a variety of things coming at your force field. These things can be both positive and negative. It could be the guy who flips you off on the freeway. It could be the husband, who says, "Yeah, honey, your new haircut looks . . . nice." It could be the children who wrinkle their noses at the meal you slaved over for an hour. It could be the parent who tries to make you feel guilty because you haven't visited in over a week. It could be someone at a networking event who looks you up and down without saying a word. It could be the person who looks bored and sighs loudly as you make your presentation. It could be the potential client who doesn't answer your repeated emails. It could be the friend who shows no interest in your business

and/or its success. It could be the clerk who is rude to you as you check out.

3. Decide whether you'll open the doors and let these things in *or* let them bounce right off your kick-butt force field and go on with your fabulous day.

You see, so many times, we don't examine what other people do and say to us before we accept it. If someone looks us up and down, we assume we've made a fashion faux pas. If someone appears to be dozing during our speech, we assume it's boring them to tears.

Do we ever consider that it could be about *them* and not *us*? What if the crabby-pants clerk just broke up with her boyfriend? What if our friend feels uncomfortable with our starting a business because they feel it shines the light on their own lack of initiative? Could all this be possible? Of course.

Since we're not mind readers (well, most of us aren't), we cannot possibly know the source of most of the things we deal with on a daily basis. Therefore, it makes a lot of sense to deflect most things.

Perhaps there's some constructive criticism that we can examine and allow in. In that case, we slide the doors open and delve into what can be changed for the good of all. Perhaps it's a sincere compliment. Then we *must* let it in.

Oftentimes, we are bad receivers. Meaning someone gives us a compliment and we brush it off saying, "Oh, this old thing? I've had it for years" or, "Well, I could have done this better but thanks." It just ricochets right off of us. We don't allow ourselves to fully enjoy appreciation from others. So when it happens, slide those force field doors wide open and let it sink in. Ahhhhhh. It feels so good.

Take Courage

So, with my force field intact, I began to share who I was. I was twice-divorced. I wasn't perfect. I was flying my freak flag. You know what? I have received some strange glances and a few glares but I've also received comments about my courage. Can you guess which ones skip off my force field and which ones are ushered inside? It's a daily part of my life now.

So the next time you find yourself with a zinger coming your way, may the force be with you.

About Laura DeTomaso Smith

Laura DeTomaso Smith is the Chief Groovy Chick at *The Breakup Lounge,* a business dedicated to helping women with broken hearts get their groovy back. As she's no stranger to heartbreak, she wants to share the knowledge and tools that she's developed to give women in the process of a divorce or at the end of a relationship a shortcut to happiness. Her warmth, compassion, and enthusiasm make her a perfect fit for women who want to take charge of their future and make it as sassy as possible!

Find out more about Laura DeTomaso Smith on her website: BreakUpLounge.com

♥

"Loving Yourself First" Note
on Restoration

"You've been walking in circles, searching. Don't drink by the water's edge. Throw yourself in. Become the water. Only then will your thirst end."

-Jeanette Berson

What is it with us entrepreneurs? So many of us rarely "turn off." We can easily fill our lives with business activity on an almost constant basis. We often watch our afternoons of work turn into late evenings of "catching up" on projects, and way too often, we get just a "whiff" of our weekends as they fly quickly by. We could work non-stop, and still not get everything done. This is our first clue as to why we have to design a better way.

I think it's great to be a passionate go-getter, but cramming more activity into your days, weeks, and months doesn't do much for your well-being or your joy level. In fact, you will get much more accomplished in your career if you give yourself some space from your work. This space is where quiet and restoration fit nicely.

I used to work closely with a successful client who was an overachiever. I coached and mentored the members in several of his business groups. He and I often traveled together for business, so I spent quite a bit of time around him. In airports, if we had even 15 minutes (and sometimes less) before our next flight, he would whip out his laptop. When we hopped in a cab for 20 blocks, his laptop was open again. The interesting thing about him was that he seemed to always be in high gear, and you could not relax with him—ever! You could feel his intensity constantly. In addition, he did not really relate well to all of his clients and colleagues. Unless there was a clear business advantage from it, he didn't usually make time for even short, general conversations.

This man was buried in what some of us know as *toxic success* (there is actually a book by Paul Pearsall written on the topic). He had let business accomplishment become his only life focus. If he would have opened a space in his life for restoration, he very likely would have found his true North again. Ironically, I recall him saying to me during lunch one day, that he envied a younger colleague—who was very successful—not because of his success, but because he often made time to go to the beach! My friend could see the need for restoration, and the appeal of it, but he just would not stop long enough to accept it for himself. No true obstacle was keeping him from decompressing and tending to his "inner man." He had the resources, and he had the team in place to take care of things for him. He could have taken an afternoon, a day, or even a week off from the intensity. Yes, he had the resources. He just did not have the mindset!

For all of our activity, and all of our running, and all of our stressing, and all of our communicating, and all of our "connecting," what do we honestly have to show for it in terms of quality of living and peace of mind? We have to think of true success as a desirable way in which to live.

I encourage you to take a good look at your life, and consider what it is all for, and what it is all about. Will that extra five or ten hours of work each week *really* make a significant difference in your bottom line? Maybe they will, but for certain, neglecting your spirit and withholding restoration from your soul will keep you from experiencing greater levels of joy and peace. Can keeping the long-term, uninterrupted tempo ever make you feel rested and whole?

It's not just workaholics who need restoration and quiet time. We all do, and we don't need restoration occasionally. We need a dose of it daily.

Restoration is as important for us as eating, sleeping, sunshine, and drinking water. It's the vitamin-packs our spirits need for health and wellness. It would be far better to let a meeting go, give up that "one last sale," or pass on an extra work day, than to neglect the regular inner rest and revitalization that we desperately and deeply need.

You renew your mind and refresh your heart when you take time to reflect and restore. Love yourself first by deliberately making restoration a regular part of your life.

Sandy Conway, the Writer of Chapter 13

Sandy is my soul sister, my Maui buddy, and someone I really adore. I met her through a mutual colleague, Steve Gutzler, one of the writers in this book. Steve and I were planning an event in Maui, and he told me that I *must* meet Sandy. He knew she and I would really hit it off. We did!

We began communicating through social media, and then by phone. Our talks were quite inspirational and long! We have so much in common. We both love God, people, music, social media, and Maui! When we visit in person or by phone, the atmosphere is so full of life! I had the chance to spend two days with Sandy at a recent event I hosted in Maui, and what a time we had. We brainstormed, conversed, shared, ate, listened to live music, laughed, and so much more, but most importantly, we grew through our time together. I think that is what makes our friendship so rich: we grow from knowing each other.

Sandy is warm like the Maui sun! She's pretty from the inside out, and on top of that she's easy going and kind. She doesn't take things too seriously, yet she knows the seriousness of a purposeful life. She has been there for me with loving support a time or two when I needed a friend, and believe me, I was so grateful for her encouragement. She's pretty good at it! I think at her very core, Sandy is an encourager. She always wants to see others lifted up.

Sandy thoroughly enjoys life, and I am so glad she lives in Maui, because she totally deserves to hang out every day in paradise! If you are ever in Maui, definitely look her up. You can find her on Facebook and Twitter, with her positive words and upbeat vibe, eager and ready to make another new friend!

Margo DeGange

♥
Chapter 13
Restoration, I'm Coming
By Sandy Conway, Social Media Queen

Aloha from Maui!

When Margo approached me about writing a chapter in this book, I felt so compelled to share with you the importance of restoration. I believe this ties in perfectly with the art and science of loving yourself first. I hope you gain wisdom as you read the importance of taking time out to restore.

I want to share with you a little about me first. I live on the North Shore of Maui, up in the rainforest of Haiku. This is a beautiful place of peace and tranquility. I call this my Garden of Eden or my little slice of heaven on earth. I have a wonderful husband who is a professional musician, two lovable dogs, and two hilarious cats. I have been blessed with so much in my life. However, I can get so focused on what I need to do in my business and life-work, that I forget to stop and just absorb my surroundings. That isn't good. That's not loving myself first.

Living here in the islands, you can get so used to your surroundings that you can sometimes take it for granted. It's something I always get to see, so I get used to it. The saying goes, "You don't know what you have until it's gone" is so true. I need to remind myself every day of what I have and how good it is. I know it sounds crazy, but when you work here for a living, you can sometimes lose yourself in your daily work and forget the importance of taking time to restore and enjoy the surroundings.

I must say I learn a lot from the tourists that come here. They are here to take a vacation and get restored. They are escaping to get away from it all. They are having fun and standing in awe of this beautiful place. They are appreciating the beauty of the island. When I take a day off for restoration, I have a personal saying, "It's good to be a tourist!"

I was inspired to write about this when my husband and I went to the beach one day. I was laying on the beach watching the tourists and taking in some sunshine. It felt good to just breathe in the salty air and feel the good vibes of my surroundings. I felt calm as I was being quiet and listening to the waves of the ocean. I was finally taking time from my busy life to restore. When it was over I felt so rejuvenated and asked myself why I don't do this more often.

I believe there is healing in restoration. It is so important for each of us to include restoration in our daily lives, so *why* don't we? We always say we need to, but when it comes down to it, we don't take time to get away. *Why* not? I believe we don't love ourselves enough when we don't take time to rejuvenate!

We must begin to factor restoration into our schedules. We gain clarity and a sense of wholeness and well-being when we run to a place of restoration!

I'm going to focus on the title of this chapter a little bit to help you understand where I'm going with this concept. In this title, "restoration" refers to a *person*. It's that *voice* that is calling out to you saying, "Come away with me." For me personally, I believe it is God's voice calling out and beckoning me to come away. There is something He wants to do in my spirit, and He can't do effectively if I'm running here, there, and everywhere. He wants me to be still and know that He is God over my life. The definition of restoration means the replacement or giving back of something lost. When we don't take time to restore, we lose our peace, joy, clarity, and balance, and we lose our effectiveness in our daily work. We need to be good to ourselves so that we can be more effective when we are helping others in our business or life-work.

The *"I'm coming"* in this title refers to our answer to "Restoration." It is saying, "Yes, I am coming *right now* so I can regain what I have lost." As I lay on the beach that day, God started speaking to me about the importance of taking time to be restored. He is my Restorer. He replaces in me everything that I need when I'm spent emotionally, physically, and spiritually; when I don't have that peace and clarity; when I have lost my joy for living; when I have "run out of juice," so to speak. In those moments, I need to love myself enough to stop and allow Him to restore me.

Now that you and I have answered the call to go and be restored, what happens next and where do we go? I don't know where you live or anything about your surroundings, but I want you to think about your most favorite place where you like to escape. Every person should have a special place where they can run away and hide for a little while. If you don't have a place, I want you to love yourself enough to go and find that special spot. It is very important that you do this. You cannot love others effectively until you first love yourself.

I'm going to take you to my favorite spot on the beach for little while. You may not be here physically, but I want you to come with me in your mind. The sand is golden, and as soft as cashmere. It feels so gentle between the toes. The ocean is as blue as a turquoise stone, and looks like a sea of glass. The wind is blowing gently through the palm trees, and every breath you take brings calmness to your spirit. All the cares of your life are melting away under the warmth of the sunshine. The ocean is as flat and calm as a lake, and there are dolphins jumping off in the distance. You can see and hear the gentle sound of the waves flowing into the shore. I want you to stop and take it all in. It is calm and peaceful here. Be drawn into this place called paradise. Be quiet and listen.

When you get to that quiet place, wherever you are, I want you to open yourself up to all that you see, smell, hear, and feel. I want you to totally relax and clear your mind. I want you to let go of the things that are burdening you. As I always say, "let go and let God." I want you to relax in this place of restoration. When I am in my special place, I get quiet and I listen to what God wants to tell me. I open myself up to what He wants to show me. In that place, He reveals to me his plan for my life. He brings clarity to my mind and reveals to me what He wants me to do next, and how He wants me to get there. He shows me His beauty and majesty in all that I see around me. He helps me to realize that I am not alone in this world, and that He is with me every step of the way. He brings peace to my soul. He brings joy to my heart. He helps me to focus on Him as I look at all the things His hands have made. All of the cares of my life melt away in His presence. I am being restored by my great Restorer.

While I am in this place with Him, I love to journal. This is something you should do, too. It will help you take in all that He wants to share with you. Journal the revelations He gives you. Meditate on them and absorb them into your spirit. This is going to help you so much. You will have something physical to take with you when you leave that place—something to use later when you want to reflect.

When you go back to your daily life after being restored, the things that God showed you aren't just for you to keep for yourself. They are for you to share with someone else. Just like when I went away to the beach that day, God gave me this message for you.

God wants you to know that He loves you and cares for you very much. He is beckoning and calling out for you to come away with Him. He wants to bring peace to your spirit. He wants to bring joy to life. He wants to reveal his perfect plan for you. He wants you to be fully restored so that you can be effective in your life-work, business, or ministry.

God wants you to love yourself first, by taking time to get away and fellowship with Him. If the Creator of the Universe cares that much about your well-being, shouldn't you do the same?

Just like the tides of the ocean, I want you to be pulled into that place of restoration, take something away from that experience, and then go share what God has given you.

Will you answer the call when you hear that voice of Restoration beckoning you in the middle of your busy day? Will you say to that voice, "I'm Coming"?

I hope you will. It will do you so much good, and it will be a blessing to those around you.

God says He will lead you beside quiet waters, but you have to follow Him to get there!

Self-Love Steps

1. Find a special quiet place you would enjoy visiting.

2. Begin to become more aware of those times when you hear the call for restoration.

3. As you start to answer the call, grab a journal or notebook, and a pen, and go to your special spot.

4. Get still and quiet and let "Restoration" speak to you.

5. Bask in the moment.

6. Make notes in your journal once you have heard what you came to hear.

7. Go and share your message with someone else.

About Sandy Conway

Sandy Conway lives in Maui, Hawaii with her wonderful husband, musician Tom Conway, two dogs, and two cats! She is an encourager, writer, podcaster, and a God-chaser! She loves helping people with the wisdom and insight God has given her! Sandy's goal in life is to bring hope and healing to a hurting world with her voice! As you listen to her messages, she wants you to be uplifted and encouraged.

Find out more about Sandy Conway on her website: SandyCMaui.com

♥

Chapter 14
The Art and Science of Loving Yourself First
By Margo DeGange, M.Ed.,
Visibility Expert and Lifestyle Designer,
International Best-Selling Author, Speaker, and Publisher

"Loving yourself first" is a concept that a lot of people have trouble embracing. Sure, most of us *do* care about ourselves, and few of us *totally* deprive self. Yes, many of us have no problem taking time out for health and fitness, or for quiet time and reflection. Yes, some of us do feel totally fine about getting our nails done or taking a vacation, but that is not entirely what I mean when I bring up the concept of "loving yourself first."

My Only Self-Love Step: Catch a Different Mindset

What I really mean when I suggest "loving yourself first" is a *new, full-bodied mindset*, and *a new way of life*. Here is my *only* first love step for you: I want you to take on a "loving yourself first" mindset from now on. Your new mindset will be based on a rich understanding of the amazing gift you have been given in being alive each day. Acknowledge this gift, and your tremendous value, and then live your life as a thankful and responsible expression of that understanding.

When you love yourself fully, there is nothing to prove to anyone, and you are free to contribute to this world, free to do your meaningful, authentic life-work, free to do things for others, and free to care about people, without doing any of it for a false sense of self-esteem or for "brownie points."

You Just Know

If you love yourself, it will show up in what you do and say. It will be evident in how you treat yourself and others. If you don't love yourself, that leaves evidence, too. When you are "all work and no play," you are not loving yourself. When you take on a client you know is a wrong fit, you are not loving yourself. When you try to do everything yourself without asking for help, you are not loving yourself. When you do lots and lots of favors, but you can't even ask for just one in return, you are not loving yourself. When you undercharge for your services or overpay for services rendered, you are not loving yourself. When you let your business or career rob you of your hobbies and time with your family and friends, you are not loving yourself. When your service to others is making you feel exhausted, so you want to quit, you are not loving yourself (and not really serving, either).

You will know whether you love yourself by how you feel everyday. If you often experience mid to high levels of frustration, exhaustion, or discouragement, that is a sign that something must change. If your life is lacking in joy, that is a wake-up alarm for you to hear and respond to.

There is no way to avoid the truth. How you treat yourself stems from what you believe about yourself, which has to do with how much value you place on your own life!

My Mini-Revelation

I used to have trouble with the "loving yourself first" concept, too. For some reason, it felt selfish, and that was partly because I didn't fully understand what loving self meant,

154

and partly because I was taught that I should always put others before myself. I too, made time for myself, but when it came to relating to others in terms of properly giving and taking, I often gave way too much, and usually failed to love myself. This carried over into my work. My beliefs in general about my "self" were not right: they were not formed from proper thinking.

We often think it is selfish to put ourselves first, and in certain contexts, it would be. It would be wrong, for example, to neglect your responsibilities to others, or abuse or use others for personal gain. It would also be wrong to be rude to another person because you only care about *your* vantage point. Loving yourself first does not mean you think only of yourself.

What I learned regarding what it meant to love myself, caused me to change the way I live, and the way I approach work, too. It helped me erect boundaries where I would not before (because I did not want to be "selfish" or because I tried to make up for my lack of self-love through overworking), and it helped me take better care of myself instead of "giving" and contributing to the point of allowing myself to be used beyond measure (spiritually, physically, emotionally, or mental). It helped me guard against too much activity and self-neglect (even when I was making sales, working out, and getting sleep).

My mini-revelation about self-love came to me one day while I was replaying in my mind the lesson many of us were taught as children—by our parents or by our teachers—which tells us to treat others as we would want them to treat us. I realized that this teaching actually stems from the well-known verse: "Love your neighbor as yourself" (Mark 12:31). In the past, as I tried to practice this principle, somehow I misunderstood the "as yourself" part of the verse, and instead, I took it to mean I should treat others *better* than I treat myself! For a long time, I believed I should always put others first and put my own needs (and desires) last, and for the most part, that is what I did.

Did I have joy from serving others while depleting myself? No, not al all. Instead, I had frustration, discouragement, and sometimes sadness, especially when I saw that many people took gross advantage, and pushed the boundaries of my willingness to give. Worse, I was actually one of the people taking advantage of my willingness to give! I took advantage of *me*! I took advantage of my own kindness, and of my ability and willingness to give and give, and to work and work, and to go far beyond the limits of what generosity and a normal, full day of work should look like. In addition, I was hard on myself, thinking I wasn't selfless enough with people, and expecting more of myself at work than was fitting. To add to the insanity, I punished myself with discouraging self-talk. You know the kind, "Why are you not further along by now?"

I experienced a lot of stress and a lack of sleep, and tiredness from too many tasks and too much daily extra activity in my life. I went from being athletic, to being someone who exercised when she could get to it. I became the once-passionate reader who never got more than two pages read before falling asleep with the book on my chest and my glasses still on my face.

As I reflected on that childhood verse, and on what it meant to be a kind and loving person who contributed to the good of the world, it hit me: I *first and foremost* must love and care for the person I am here to be. I saw so clearly that there is *no one else* in this world placed here to take full care of me, but *me!*

I began to really understand how much of a gift my life is, and how important it is that I nurture and care for that life, as if it were my own child! *I* was the caretaker—the *only* caretaker—of this particular living being. I was *the one assigned* to take care of this being, called *me!*

I Finally saw what that verse really meant. I should *love myself!* I should love myself *fully,* like I mean it! I should love myself like I am *thankful that I am alive!* I should love myself because I have been *entrusted* with the care of myself!

I began to get the picture that when I am solidly on the self-love path, I can love others with a love that is true. I can serve the world from a place of empowerment. I can care about my family, friends, and clients from the perspective of true giving. We test drive God's love on ourselves, then we take it to the road called "others," and let it rip! It is not until we love ourselves that our authentic service really begins!

Being Poured Out in a Good Way

When we love ourselves first, we *will* serve. Still, service takes effort. It's full of potholes and bumps, even when we're doing it right. In our work, there will certainly be times when we feel poured out, and that's O.K. It is all part of serving. It's important though, that in our commitment to love ourselves first, we recognize when we start to feel low on fuel or depleted. If we have a headache, we should rest, and not call five more clients. If we don't get proper sleep one night, we should get good sleep the very next day, letting something else go. We should know when to serve and when to refresh ourselves. It is not meant for us to "do it all". We are not here to save the world; we are here to help a small part of it. That can only happen when we are taking very good care of ourselves.

It is my desire to spark your desire—through the pages of this book—to love yourself first, and become fully alive in this experience we call life. We are so blessed to be here, in *this* day, having *this* human experience. I encourage you to let your life and your life-work become a "thank-you" message and a love-letter! Practice the art and science of loving yourself first, 'cause your business should never deplete you. Instead, it should empower and complete you.

About Margo DeGange

Business and Lifestyle Designer Margo DeGange, M.Ed., is an international best-selling author and sought-after speaker, and the founder of the exciting mentoring and collaborative network, *Women of Splendor,* where spiritually-minded women with businesses and important life-work discover and develop their brilliance; increase their reach and visibility; and bring healing to the world in a BIG and splendid way. Margo is also the founder of *Splendor Publishing,* offering experts in many areas the opportunity to become published authors quickly and with ease. Known as *The Visibility Expert*, Margo helps entrepreneurs, ministers, and individuals discover their "Gift of Brilliance" and shine FULL THROTTLE!

Find out more about Margo DeGange on her website: MargoDeGange.com

Is there a book in you, waiting to spring forth?
We'd love to help you become a published author!

Splendor Publishing helps entrepreneurs, ministers, and individuals with important life-work become published authors. Our books are written by experts who want to share their big and brilliant message with the world!

Splendor books encourage personal, professional, and spiritual growth. Let us help you make your dream of being a published author a reality. Contact *Splendor Publishing* today: **SplendorPublishing.com**

Made in the USA
Charleston, SC
25 August 2013